Picture it in Needlepoint

Ben's Room Door Plaque

Picture it in Needlepoint

Judy Clayton & Deborah Dow

David & Charles

Thatched Cottage
Page 2 Benjamin Sampler

A DAVID & CHARLES BOOK

Copyright Text, designs and charts © Judy Clayton & Deborah Dow 1993
Photography © David & Charles 1993

First published 1993

Judy Clayton & Deborah Dow have asserted their rights to be identified as authors of this work in accordance with the Copyright, Designs and Patents Act 1988.

All rights reserved. No part of this publication may be reproduced, stored in a retrieval system, or transmitted, in any form or by any means, electronic or mechanical, by photocopying, recording or otherwise, without prior permission in writing from the publisher.

A catalogue record for this book is available from the British Library.

ISBN 0 7153 0007 5

Typeset by ABM Typographics Ltd, Hull
and printed in England
by Butler & Tanner Ltd, Frome
for David & Charles
Brunel House Newton Abbot Devon

CONTENTS

Introduction	6
Acknowledgements	8

1 Basic Techniques 9

2 Greetings Cards 16
Cat on a Windowledge
Country Scene
Georgian Country House
Hollyhocks
Heartfelt Greetings
Happy Birthday
New Arrival
Teddy and Balloons

3 Christmas 30
Christmas Bow
Twinkling Star
Robin on a Snowy Bough
Christmas Goose
Christmas Tree
Christmas Cat
Ho! Ho! Ho!
Christmas Wreath

4 The Nursery 46
Jennifer's Fairy
Benjamin's Sampler and Door Plaque
Emma's Swans and Rabbits
Alphabet Cushion
Teddy Bears' Picnic

5 Victorian Treasures 66
Canterbury Bells
Pansy and Red Campion
Pink Poppies
Thatched Cottage
Victorian Posy Box
Butterfly Needlecase
Butterfly Pincushion

6 Decorative Ideas 84
Floral Frame
Picture Bow
Hair Bow
Country Cottage Pot Pourri

7 Special Occasions and Mementoes 100
Wedding Sampler
Home Sweet Home
Celebration Floral Wreath

8 Exotica 112
Blue Macaw
Tropical Cushion
Oriental Fish
Two Plump Penguins

Borders and Alphabets 126

Index 128

INTRODUCTION

THERE are more than forty appealing needlepoint projects in this book, with easy designs to entice the novice needleworker and more challenging projects for the experienced stitcher, including a wealth of different themes, from special celebrations and Christmas ideas to decorative and period pieces for the home. All these colourful projects are stitched in stranded cotton (floss) on canvas, using simple continental tent stitch, and occasionally a few other stitches to create depth and detail. Technicalities have been kept to a minimum as we believe that needlework should always be pleasurable and relaxing. Chapter 1 gives all the necessary information on basic techniques, materials, mounting and framing and should be read before starting any project. Above all, do not worry about mistakes. They are inevitable and frequently do not really matter. You are allowed a little creative licence in a design; such things add a more personal touch.

Our designs are usually quite small, yet full of detail. They are quick, inexpensive to work and good for boosting confidence. Most needlepointers have started a large project with enthusiasm but it often ends up abandoned in a cupboard unfinished! Since so many people today lead such busy lives, we felt that there was an opportunity for a collection of designs that can be tucked into a bag and worked on whenever time and circumstances permit. Youngsters who like stitching will enjoy the contemporary, easy-to-sew designs with their bold colours.

Needlepoint becomes addictive. On finishing a project, your fingers will itch to start the next and you will be able to dip into this book time and time again as occasions occur throughout the year. Each project is beautifully photographed, has a full-colour chart and a colour list giving DMC and Anchor stranded cotton (floss) numbers. Easy-to-follow instructions and diagrams guide you through every step of the project, from placing the first stitches to adding the finishing touches. Many designs can be adapted by changing colours or adding decorative or personal motifs and lettering. You will soon be adding ideas of your own!

Oriental Fish

We began our stitching careers by making birth samplers for customers of our former children's clothes shop who were looking for unusual christening and birthday gifts. We soon found that the demand for these samplers was outstripping our expectations. This sideline eventually developed into our company. Thumbelina Designs produces small needlepoint kits using designs similar to the ones featured in this book. They are available from many needlework shops and department stores nationwide. Inspiration has also been drawn from our interest in the decorative arts, particularly the ceramics, textiles and stationery of Victorian times.

We have taken enormous pleasure in compiling the projects in this book, not only in the designing and stitching, but also in the search for ideas. Inspiration has come from surprising sources such as tea cosies found in junk shops, Victorian paper scraps found in the attic, and ceramic tiles from old fireplaces and doorways. We hope that you enjoy working the designs as much as we have and that you too will be inspired to create your own personal designs. Keep stitching!

Further information on Thumbelina Designs can be obtained from Thumbelina Designs, The Courtyard, Evelyn Road, Chiswick, London W4 5JL.

US READERS

We have included in round brackets () US terms for words which otherwise may be confusing to North American readers.

ACKNOWLEDGEMENTS

This book would never have been completed without the help and support of the backup team. Our grateful thanks go to Vivienne Wells and Maggi McCormick and everyone at David and Charles for their professional help and guidance. To Pat Blacker and Jo Wallace for deciphering and typing. To Brenda and Terry Menin for stitching and creative input and to Simon Clayton for his patience and cooperation. We would especially like to thank Amanda Hutchinson, Fraser Blackburn and Esmond Reid for their encouragement and enthusiasm in getting this book started.

But it is to our families and friends that we say our biggest thank you, for their unfailing encouragement and tolerance has kept us going.

CHAPTER 1

Basic Techniques

MATERIALS AND EQUIPMENT

Canvas

Canvas made specifically for needlepoint is constructed from an even mesh of horizontal and vertical threads. As well as canvas made from cotton, which was used to make the projects in this book, canvas is available in linen, silk and plastic. Plastic canvas is particularly good for children to use as the holes are large and easier to work.

There are two types of canvas. *Single, or mono, interlocked canvas* has single threads, horizontal and vertical, woven under and over each other, and into each other at every junction. *Double interlocked canvas*, which is sometimes called *Penelope*, has pairs of threads running vertically and horizontally.

The projects in this book are all worked on single canvas. Canvas is *graded* by the number of holes to the inch or centimetre. The finer the canvas, the more holes there are to the inch/cm. Most of the designs in this book are worked on canvas with 18 holes to the inch/ 7 to the cm. If the canvas has more holes to the inch/cm, the finished design will be smaller and vice versa.

Always buy good-quality canvas. Cheaper versions may have broken threads, knots or an uneven weave which will distort the finished design. Different colours are available. White is preferable for designs with large areas of pale background colour.

Leave a border of canvas around your work at least 1–½ inches/4cm wide and seal the edges of larger pieces with masking tape to prevent the canvas from fraying or catching the thread.

Needles

Needlepoint should be worked with tapestry needles, which are usually blunt. They are available in different numbered sizes; the finer the needle, the higher the number. The needle should pass through the canvas easily without pushing the threads apart and the eye should be held in place by the canvas threads without allowing the needle to fall through. For example, use a No 22 tapestry needle on 18-hole canvas and a No 20 on 14-hole canvas.

Most needles are made of steel and they tarnish and snag with use. Discard them if they become rough – they can catch and damage the canvas and the thread.

Gold-plated and even platinum needles are now available in many needlework shops. They slide through the canvas with less friction and they will not rust or mark the canvas.

Threads

The projects in this book are all worked in stranded cottons (floss), which are made up of six strands and are available in 8¾ yard/8 metre skeins. There are hundreds of colours to choose from. Most threads are colourfast but test them before you try to clean them.

Two other kinds of threads have been used to enhance the projects here. Cotton perlé (pearl cotton) No 5 is a twisted rope-like thread with a silky sheen. It has been used for outlining motifs and to create a raised effect. Metallic threads, used to give sparkle in many of the designs, are now widely available but vary enormously in quality. We have specified the particular make on the colour chart where relevant. Some types may tend to split, so use short lengths of 10 inches/25cm to help prevent this from happening.

Frames

Many of the designs in this book are small enough to work without a tapestry frame. In fact, we work almost all of our needlepoint 'in the hand', which means without a frame. However, it is highly recommended that larger designs be worked in a frame to prevent distortion, and people who are used to working with a frame will find it more comfortable.

Frames can be either floor-standing or hand-held. They vary greatly in size, construction and quality. When buying one, look particularly at the smoothness of the wood and the free running of the screw adjustments.

A frame consists of two horizontal rollers with tapes onto which the needlework is sewn. These rollers slot into two vertical stretchers and are held in place by screws and bolts. The canvas is then laced to the stretchers (Fig 1).

To get used to using a frame before starting a design, work a few stitches at the edge of the canvas. You should be able to push the needle up through the canvas with one hand and down with the other.

Other materials

Graph paper is essential if you are creating your own design. It is available as ordinary squared paper or as tracing paper which can be placed over a picture or motif that you want to copy exactly.

Masking tape is used to bind canvas edges to prevent threads from catching.

Scissors should be medium-sized and sharp for cutting and trimming canvas and backing fabrics, and small and pointed for cutting threads. Do not use either pair for cutting paper or they will blunt very quickly.

STARTING AND FINISHING NEEDLEPOINT

Getting comfortable

Make sure you work in good light, preferably daylight, especially when using fine canvas. Lightbulbs which simulate daylight provide the most natural light under which to work. Specialist magnifying glasses and lamps are also available from many needlework shops.

Keep your hands and working area clean. Light-coloured threads will show up any dirt.

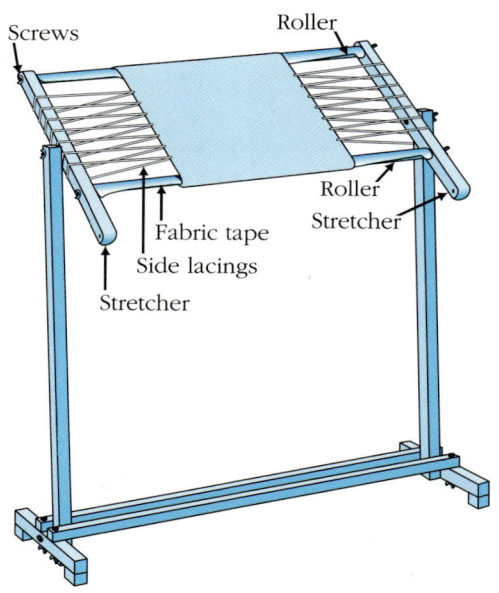

Fig 1 Free-standing tapestry frame

Starting to stitch

To begin your needlepoint design, fold the canvas in half and then in half again to find the centre. Mark this point with a fabric marker. Then find the centre point on the chart. If this is not marked, count the number of stitches along one vertical side and one horizontal side and divide each by two (Fig 2). Then work colour by colour from this central point. It may be easier to start with a particular motif near the centre, especially if the centre point falls on an area of solid background colour.

20 inches/50cm for large areas of background colour. Do not be tempted to use longer lengths as they will tangle and knot.

Begin each row of colour by pushing the needle up through the canvas. Hold the end of the thread underneath and sew over it with your first few stitches. Do not knot the thread as this will leave unsightly bumps under the finished work (Fig 3).

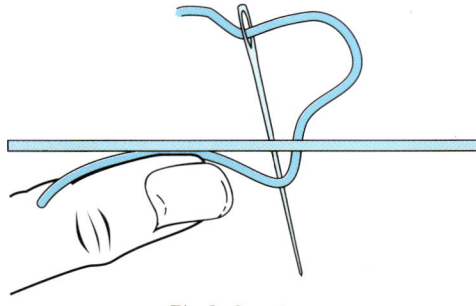

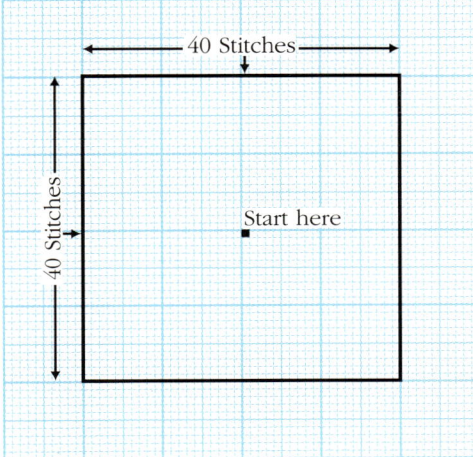

Fig 3 Starting

Fig 2 How to find a centre point

Stitch areas of colour rather than working row by row. If two areas of the same colour are close together, you can jump across a few stitches. Otherwise finish off the thread and start again.

To finish, push the needle through the last few stitches on the reverse side of the work and cut off the thread neatly (Fig 4). Check the number of stitches worked against the chart carefully. It is easier to unpick any mistakes if the back of the work is neat.

To start, separate the strands of cotton (floss) and then combine three strands together. This helps keep the threads from twisting around each other as you stitch. If more or less strands are used in a project, this will be indicated in the colour code. On designs with a dark background, four or five strands give a fuller covering. In some designs two threads of one colour and one thread of a second colour are used to give a mottled or shaded effect. This will also be indicated in the colour code, eg 676 x 2, 680 x 1 means use 2 strands of light ochre 676 and 1 strand of dark ochre 680 in your needle.

Save all remaining threads for use later. Cut lengths of threads approximately 15 inches/40cm long for working details and motifs, and

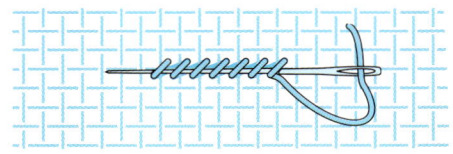

Fig 4 Finishing

NEEDLEPOINT STITCHES

In needlepoint the whole canvas is worked, leaving no unstitched areas. There are dozens of needlepoint stitches, some more decorative and detailed than others. This book concentrates on tent stitch. Backstitch, French knots, brick stitch and sloping Gobelin stitch are used to provide outline detail and texture.

Continental tent stitch

Tent stitch can be worked from left to right or right to left, vertically or horizontally. It should be stitched in two movements: push the needle up through the canvas first and then down into the next hole.

To work from left to right pass the needle up through square 1 and down through square 2, then back up through square 3 and down through square 4. To work from right to left pass the needle up through 1 and down through 2; continue up through 3 and down through 4 (Fig 5). A long diagonal stitch will be formed on the reverse side of the canvas. Do not go up and down in one motion as this will pull the canvas out of shape. With all diagonal stitches, it is important to get the tension right or the canvas will be distorted. Practise a few stitches on a spare piece of canvas before you begin working your design.

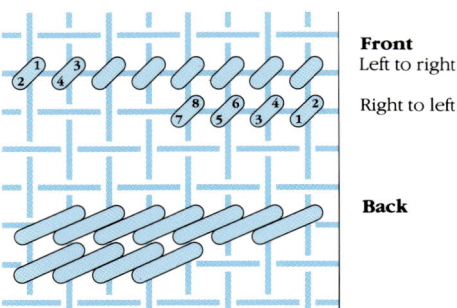

Fig 5 Continental tent stitch

The threads may twist during stitching. Allow the needle to hang down from the work and the threads will unwind themselves.

If your finished piece looks lopsided, it can be gently pulled back into shape, or 'blocked' (see Mounting and framing, page 14).

There are two other methods of working tent stitch. Half cross stitch uses less thread but leaves only a short vertical or horizontal stitch on the reverse. It is not as hardwearing as con- tinental tent stitch and we do not recommend using it. Diagonal tent stitch does not distort the canvas and is ideal for covering large areas of background. It is worked in diagonal rows starting with a stitch in the top right-hand corner. Pass the needle up through square 1, down through square 2, up through square 3 and so on. The reverse side of the work appears to be 'woven', hence its other name, Basketweave tent stitch (Fig 6).

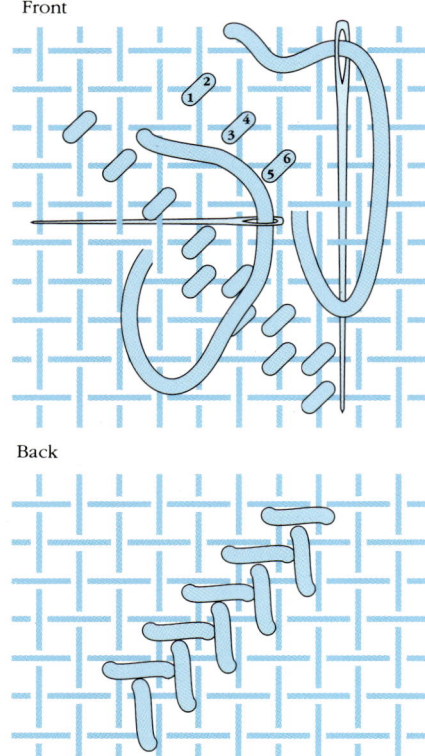

Fig 6 Diagonal (Basketweave) tent stitch

Brick stitch

This stitch is useful for background areas and gives a textured appearance particularly suitable for roofs, sea or landscapes. It is a straight stitch worked over an even number of threads of canvas. It can be worked over 2, 3 or 4 threads, vertically or horizontally. Work the first row of stitches and then fit the subsequent rows into the gaps left by the previous row.

Come up at 1 and down into 2, up at 3 and down into 4 and so on (Fig 7). Small compensatory stitches will be needed to fill in the gaps to cover the area completely.

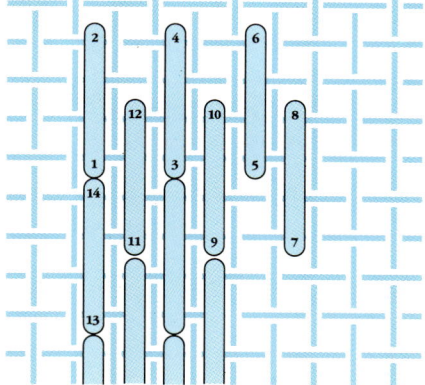

Fig 7 Brick stitch

Backstitch

This is used to outline areas of colour using one strand of thread. Pass the needle up through square 1, down through square 2, up through square 3, and so on (Fig 8). You will have a double length stitch on the reverse side of the work. Backstitch can be worked in any direction. Complete all the tent stitch areas before working backstitch outlines.

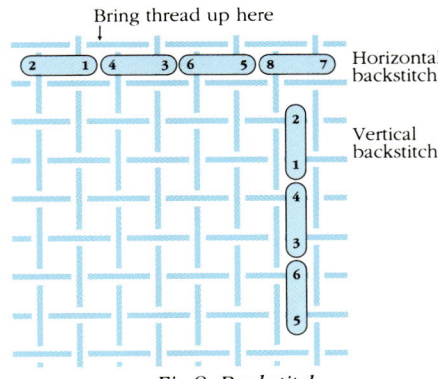

Fig 8 Backstitch

Sloping Gobelin stitch

This is another useful filling stitch to provide texture. It is worked over 2, 3 or 4 diagonal intersections of the canvas. Pass the needle up through square 1, down through square 2, up through square 3, and so on (Fig 9). Make sure that the stitches all slant in the same direction when you are working the stitch as the border to a design.

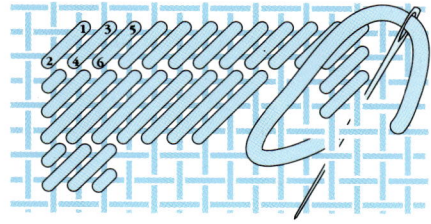

Fig 9 Sloping Gobelin stitch

French knots

French knots are used decoratively to make flowers and accentuate small details. Bring the thread up through the square. Wrap the thread around the needle once (twice for a large knot) and pass the needle down into a hole adjacent to where the thread comes up (Fig 10). Pull the needle through carefully, allowing the thread to form a knot on the surface.

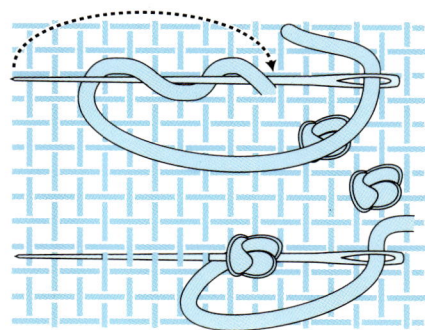

Fig 10 French knots

Oversewing

Some projects require a few stitches which you must oversew. This means taking a long single stitch from one given point to another, usually as a single strand, for example to make a cat's whiskers or blades of grass.

FOLLOWING THE CHART AND COLOUR CODE

Each square on the chart generally indicates one stitch. On the colour code on each chart, the coloured symbols are shown next to the DMC colour numbers. If different shades of one colour are used, a different symbol is shown for each one. Equivalent Anchor numbers are listed in the chart key at the end of the project instructions, but they are not necessarily identical colours.

Please note: The charts are not shown actual size, so it it not possible to place the chart behind the canvas as a guide.
On each chart:
Tent stitch is shown as a block of colour.
Backstitch is shown as a solid line around areas of colour.
Brick stitch is shown as a solid line of colour through the centre of the relevant squares.
French knots are indicated on the colour code relating to the design.

Although the chart key includes both DMC and Anchor thread numbers, threads from other manufacturers may correspond to the colours indicated. Provided they are of equal quality, similar results will be achieved. Where relevant, instructions specific to a particular design will be included in the colour code.

You will need a maximum of 1 skein of stranded cotton (floss) for each colour listed, unless otherwise stated.

Measurements for the size of canvas needed and the finished projects are approximate.

GRAPHING LETTERS AND NUMBERS

A number of the projects in this book are greetings cards and samplers on which you can stitch names or initials and dates to personalise the piece and commemorate an important event. The simplest way to do this is to chart the letters and numbers that you need on a piece of graph paper. There are a number of alphabets in the book which chart the squares required for each letter or number. First choose the letters you need and draw them on graph paper, or count the total number of stitches in the name including one stitch space between each letter. Count the total number of stitches across the width of the design. Make sure you count inside the border if there is one. Deduct the name total from the width total and then divide the resulting figure by two. This gives the exact number of stitch spaces on each side of the name. For example, if there are five spaces on each side, start stitching on the sixth stitch.

Position a date or number in the same way, but allow three stitches between the day, month and year. To position initials only, as on the Celebration Wreath, leave three stitches between each letter.

MOUNTING AND FRAMING

Mounting cards

All the cards in this book have been mounted on 3-fold cards with a variety of shaped 'windows', now widely available in most craft and needlework shops. To mount your finished needlework, trim the canvas from the edge of the needlepoint approximately 3/8 inches/1cm all around. Fit it into the window opening in section B (Fig 11a) and mount it using white craft (PVA) glue, spray mount or double-sided tape. Place the needlework right side down on the table and fold section A over section B (Fig 11b). Secure it with glue or tape. Before gluing section A in place you can insert a piece of folded paper cut to size behind the needlework on which to write your message (Fig 11c). Place the finished card under a weight to make sure it sticks firmly.

Blocking and mounting pictures

When your needlework is finished it will need stretching to pull it back into shape. This is called blocking. You will need a clean, smooth, thick board large enough to hold your canvas,

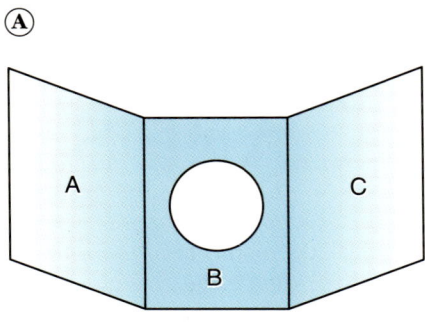

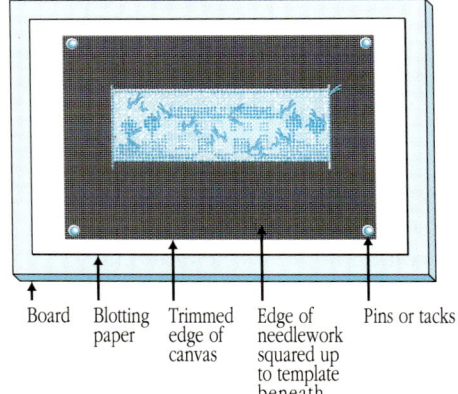

Fig 12 Blocking

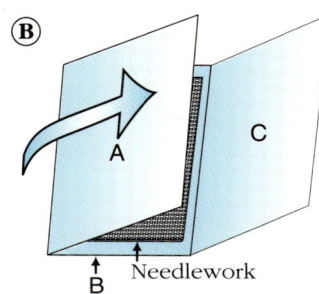

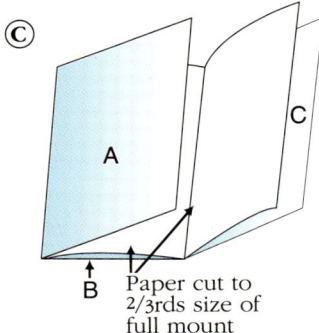

Fig 11 Three-fold mount card

thin cardboard, tacks or pins to secure the canvas, and a piece of thin cloth.

First make a template of the outline of the design on a piece of thin cardboard or blotting paper and secure it to the board. Place your needlework face down on the template. Secure one corner with a tack or pin. Use a steam iron to dampen the work lightly and gently pull the remaining corners out to fit the template and pin them down (Fig 12). Place the cloth over the work and press softly with the iron. Barely touch the work – pressing hard will flatten the stitches. Gradually the stitches will be pulled back into shape. Do not unpin the piece from the board until it is completely dry. Leave for at least 24 hours.

Frames

Ready made frames are widely available in a vast range of sizes and materials. If you find one you like, allow about 1½ to 2 inches (4 to 5cm) around the work as a border. A professional picture framer can cut a card mount (mat board) the colour you choose. If you have an antique frame you want to use, a frame shop should be able to supply backing board, mount hooks and cord as well.

Custom-made frames can be assembled from a large selection of picture mouldings to complement any design. Materials include wood and bamboo – plain, gilded, lacquered, or painted – and different coloured and finished metals. It is worth spending a little time researching different materials as the finished frame can make a tremendous difference to the way a piece looks.

Glass, in spite of its transparency, obscures some of the texture when it is used in needlework frames. The framed pictures in this book have not been covered with glass, but in some cases where protection is needed, it may be preferable to use glass. If so, the work should be mounted and framed with spacers so that the glass does not touch the stitches.

CHAPTER 2

GREETINGS CARDS

THERE is always an occasion to take or send a card, and one that is chosen with care and attention is always highly valued. People have been giving and receiving cards for centuries. Often containing simple greetings or romantic verses, they were traditionally made at home and handed over in person. Nowadays the card industry is big business and it is increasingly difficult to find a way of sending an original greeting. Creating your own card is one way to personalise the message.

Many of the projects in this chapter can be adapted or made more personal by, for example, changing the colour of the wallpaper, or the cat on the windowledge, or the baby's crib. A variety of alphabets are provided so that you can place any initial on your piece.

Stitched cards can be sent on any special occasion – birthdays, anniversaries, Valentine's Day, Mother's Day, Easter – and of course Christmas, to which we've devoted an entire chapter. Greet the arrival of a new baby or offer wedding congratulations, say hello to a special friend far away, or send best wishes to the proud owner of a new house.

A variety of mount cards are available with different sized and shaped windows. If you want to use a different card from the one in a project shown, you may need to stitch an extra border, or more or less background. There is a wide choice of colours, textures and finishes, including embossed, metallic and marbled. Some cards have greetings already printed on them, or you could handwrite a message using a gold or silver pen. Cards can also be embellished with ribbons or tiny silk flowers or tassels. Use very fine satin ribbon for a delicate effect.

Black Cat on Windowledge and Teddy and Balloons Cards

CAT ON A WINDOWLEDGE

Send this card to wish a special person 'Good Luck'.

NEEDLE Size 22
CANVAS 18 holes per inch (7 holes per cm)
SIZE OF CANVAS 5 x 5in (127 x 127mm)
SIZE OF FINISHED DESIGN 2½ x 2½in (64 x 64mm)
☐ Stranded cottons (floss) listed on chart key
☐ Mount card 3-fold white parchment with pre-cut 2½in (64mm) square window

1 Find the centre point on the canvas and position the design as described in Basic Techniques.
2 Count the number of stitches from the centre point to the cat's head and start stitching here. Then work colour by colour.
3 Oversew the cat's whiskers using 1 strand of black 310 thread as indicated on the chart.
4 Mount the card following the instructions in Basic Techniques.

DMC	COLOUR	ANCHOR
742	Gold	303
800	Pale Blue	128
310	Black	403
798	Blue	131
954	Light Green	203
700	Bright Green	228
744	Yellow	295
321	Burgundy	47
666	Red	46
Blanc	White	01

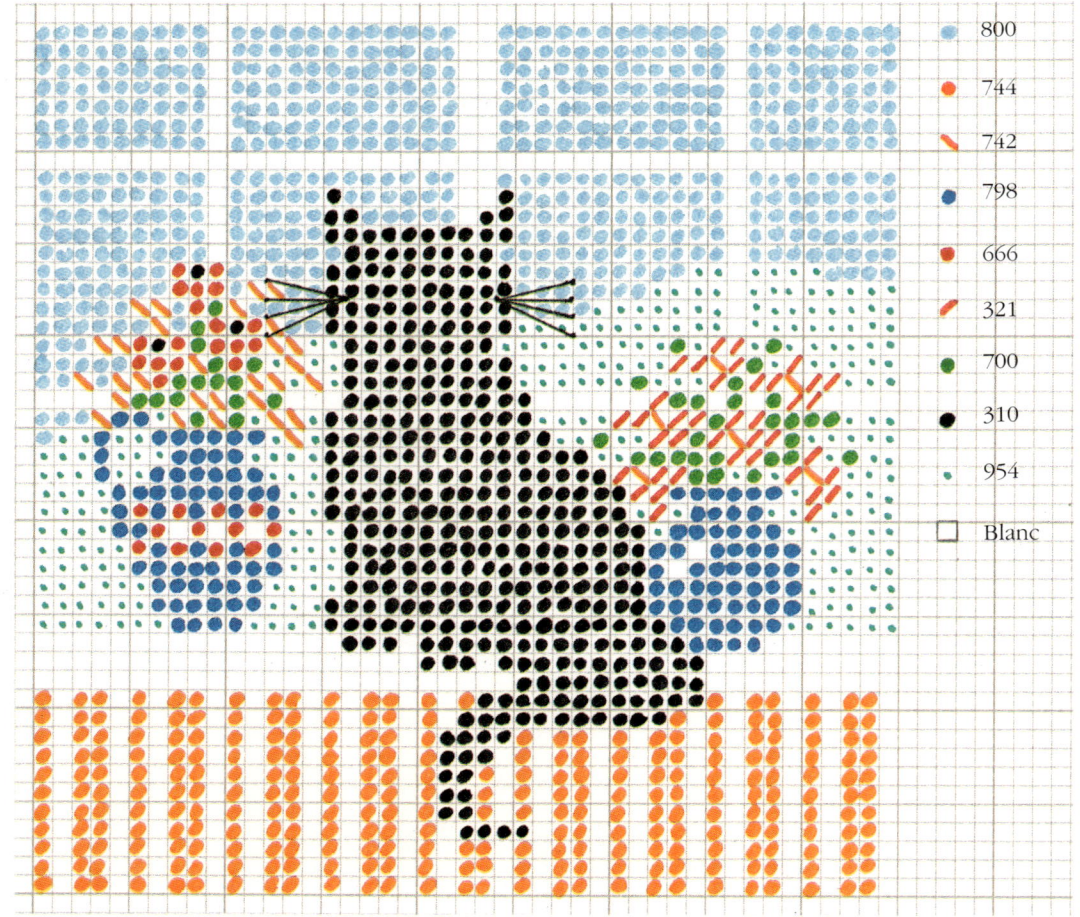

COUNTRY SCENE

This little card could be sent on any occasion, possibly to say thank you or just as a simple greeting. It could also be mounted and framed as a miniature picture.

NEEDLE Size 22
CANVAS 18 holes per inch (7 holes per cm)
SIZE OF CANVAS 4½ x 4½in (115 x 115mm)
SIZE OF FINISHED DESIGN 2½ x 2½in (64 x 64mm)
- Mount card 3-fold white parchment with pre-cut 2½in (64mm) square windows
- Stranded cottons (floss) as listed on chart key

1 Find the centre point on the canvas and position the design as described in Basic Techniques.
2 Count the numbers of stitches from the centre point to the bottom horizontal line of the fence and start stitching here.
3 Build up the picture by sewing the sheep, trees and foliage before filling in the fields and other background details.
4 Mount the card following the instructions in Basic Techniques.

DMC	COLOUR	ANCHOR
3346	Dark Green	267
3347	Green	266
3348	Pale Green	265
471	Mid Green	254
3345	Very Dark Green	268
744	Pale Yellow	295
746	Cream	386
743	Yellow	305
310	Black	403
208	Purple	110
800	Pale Blue	128
309	Pink	39
3031	Dark Brown	386
300	Brown	352
301	Rust	349
Blanc	White	01

GEORGIAN COUNTRY HOUSE

This elegant house set in a cottage garden would be suitable for someone moving to a new home or for a birthday.

NEEDLE Size 22
CANVAS 18 holes per inch (7 holes per cm)
SIZE OF CANVAS 5½ x 5½in (140 x 140mm)
SIZE OF FINISHED DESIGN 3¼ x 3¼in (80 x 80mm)
☐ Stranded cottons (floss) listed on chart key
☐ Mount card 3-fold white parchment with 3¼in (80mm) pre-cut square window

1 Find the centre point on the canvas and position the design as described in Basic Techniques.
2 Count the number of stitches from the centre point to the front door of the house and start stitching here. Work colour by colour. Work the roof and path in Brick Stitch.
3 When the design is complete outline in backstitch using 1 strand of dark grey 317 for the windows and top of the door, and 1 strand of black 310 around the door.

Georgian House, Hollyhocks and Country Scene Cards

4   With 1 strand of white work long stitches over the windows to make panes.

5   Mount the card following the instructions in Basic Techniques. If you wish, you can add a pretty ribbon rose, which can be purchased already made.

DMC	COLOUR	ANCHOR
Blanc	White	01
310	Black	403
317	Dark Grey	400
415	Light Grey	398

DMC	COLOUR	ANCHOR
746	Cream	386
772	Pale Green	253
3347	Green	266
3346	Mid Green	267
936	Dark Green	846
300	Brown	352
666	Red	46
208	Purple	110
744	Yellow	295
742	Gold	303
335	Pink	41
798	Dark Blue	131
800	Light Blue	128

HOLLYHOCKS

This pretty card is suitable for a birthday, Mother's Day or perhaps Easter.

NEEDLE Size 22
CANVAS 18 holes per inch (7 holes per cm)
SIZE OF CANVAS 5 x 6in (125 x 150mm)
SIZE OF FINISHED DESIGN 2¼ x 3in (57 x 76mm)
☐ Stranded cottons (floss) listed on the chart key
☐ Mount card 3-fold card with 2¼ x 3in (57 x 76mm) pre-cut window

1 Find the centre point on the canvas and position the design as described in Basic Techniques.
2 Count the stitches from the centre point to the base of the tallest hollyhock and start stitching here.
3 When the design is complete outline the white fence using backstitch and 1 strand of grey 317.
4 Oversew the back fence using 1 strand of brown 300.
5 Mount the card following the instructions in Basic Techniques.

DMC	COLOUR	ANCHOR
Blanc	White	01
317	Grey	400
300	Brown	352
794	Blue	129
208	Purple	110
210	Pale Purple	104
702	Bright Green	226
699	Dark Green	923
772	Light Green	253
742	Gold	303
321	Burgundy	47
335	Pink	41
3326	Pale Pink	25
729	Ochre	890
676	Pale Ochre	891

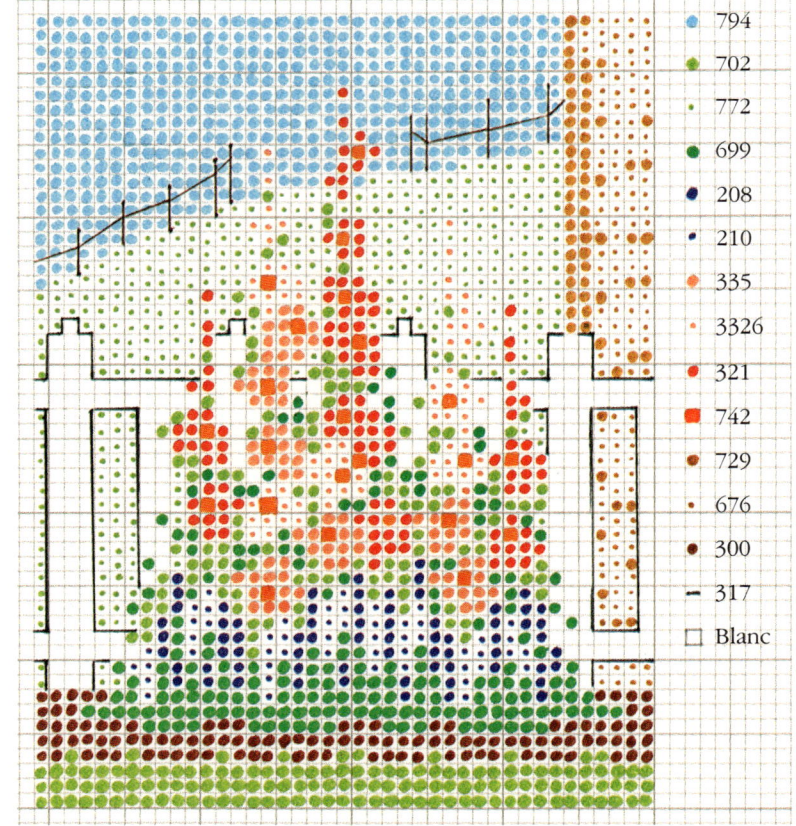

22

HEARTFELT GREETINGS

You can work this pretty card in other colours. Choose three shades of the colour you prefer and exchange them for the pinks on the chart.

NEEDLE Size 22
CANVAS 18 holes per inch (7 holes per cm)
SIZE OF CANVAS 5 x 5in (127 x 127mm)
SIZE OF FINISHED DESIGN 2½ x 2½in (64 x 64mm)
- Stranded cottons (floss) as listed on the chart key
- Mount card 3-fold card with pre-cut heart-shaped window 2½in (64mm) from top to bottom points

1 Find the centre point on the canvas and position the design as described in Basic Techniques.
2 Count the number of stitches from the centre point to the top of the bow. Start stitching here working colour by colour.
3 Work initials in the centre in your choice of colours using the alphabet on page 127. Make sure there are an equal number of stitches on each side.
4 Work the background in white. If the heart window on your card is larger than suggested, add more background stitches.
5 Outline the bow using backstitch and 1 strand of burgundy 321. Mount the card following the instructions in Basic Techniques.

DMC	COLOUR	ANCHOR
Blanc	White	01
3346	Dark Green	267
335	Dark Pink	41
899	Pink	52
3326	Light Pink	25
321	Burgundy	47

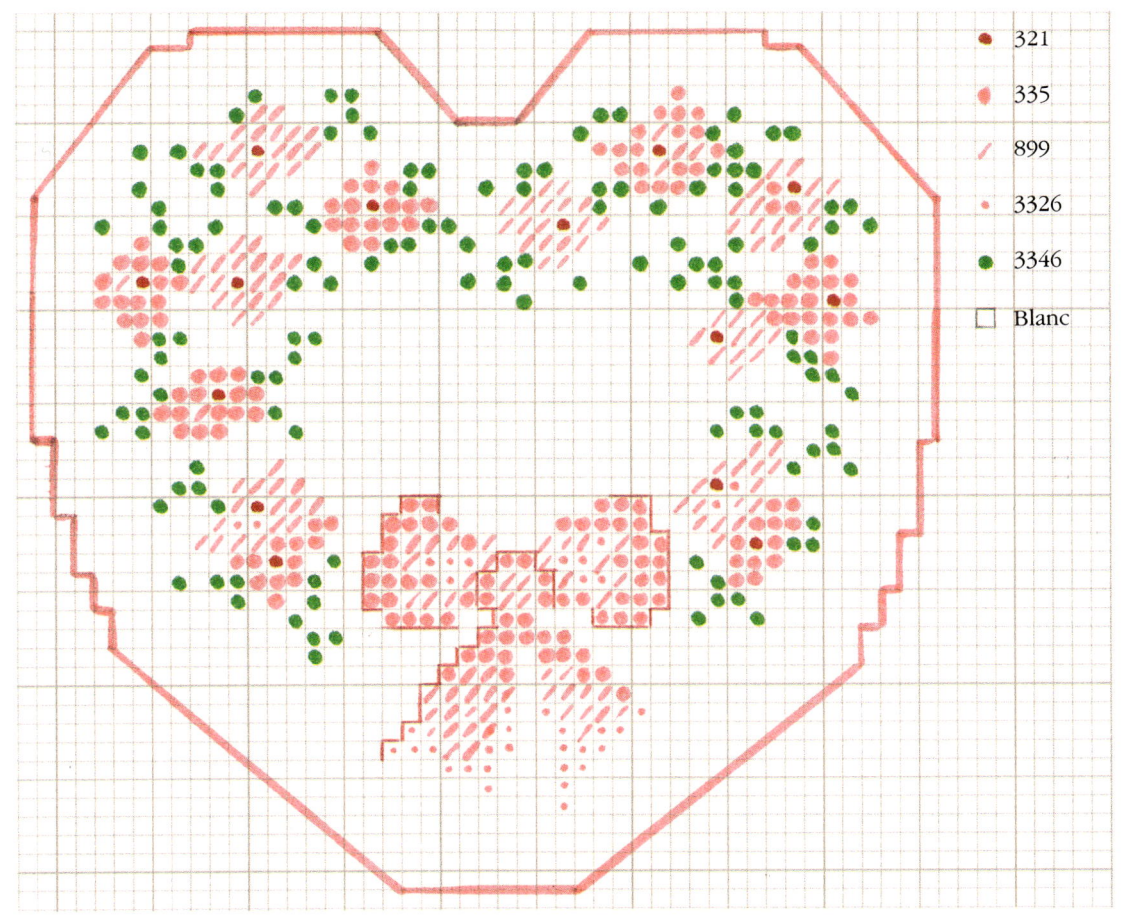

23

HAPPY BIRTHDAY

The metallic threads make this card fun to work.

NEEDLE Size 22
CANVAS 18 holes per inch (7 holes per cm)
SIZE OF CANVAS 4½ x 4½in (115 x 115mm)
SIZE OF FINISHED DESIGN 2½ x 2½in (64 x 64mm)
- Stranded cottons (floss) and metallic threads as listed on the chart key
- Mount card 3-fold white parchment card with 2½in (64mm) pre-cut window

1 Find the centre point on the canvas and position the design as described in Basic Techniques.
2 Count from the centre point to the top pink border of the cake, start stitching here. Work the cake colour by colour, then work the other objects. Using 1 strand of pink 309, backstitch the top of the cake following the pink lines on the chart.
3 Stitch the background. Oversew the yellow present with a cross of metallic gold 325.
4 Mount the card following the instructions in Basic Techniques.

DMC	COLOUR	ANCHOR
954	Light Green	203
3345	Dark Green	268
3346	Mid Green	267
666	Red	46
744	Yellow	295
743	Dark Yellow	305
742	Gold	303
310	Black	403
800	Pale Blue	128
899	Pink	52
309	Dark Pink	39
798	Blue	131
746	Cream	386
700	Bright Green	228
Blanc	White	01
MADEIRA	Metallic Gold	325
KREINIK BALGER Fine Braid 8:		
	Red	003
	Blue	051HL

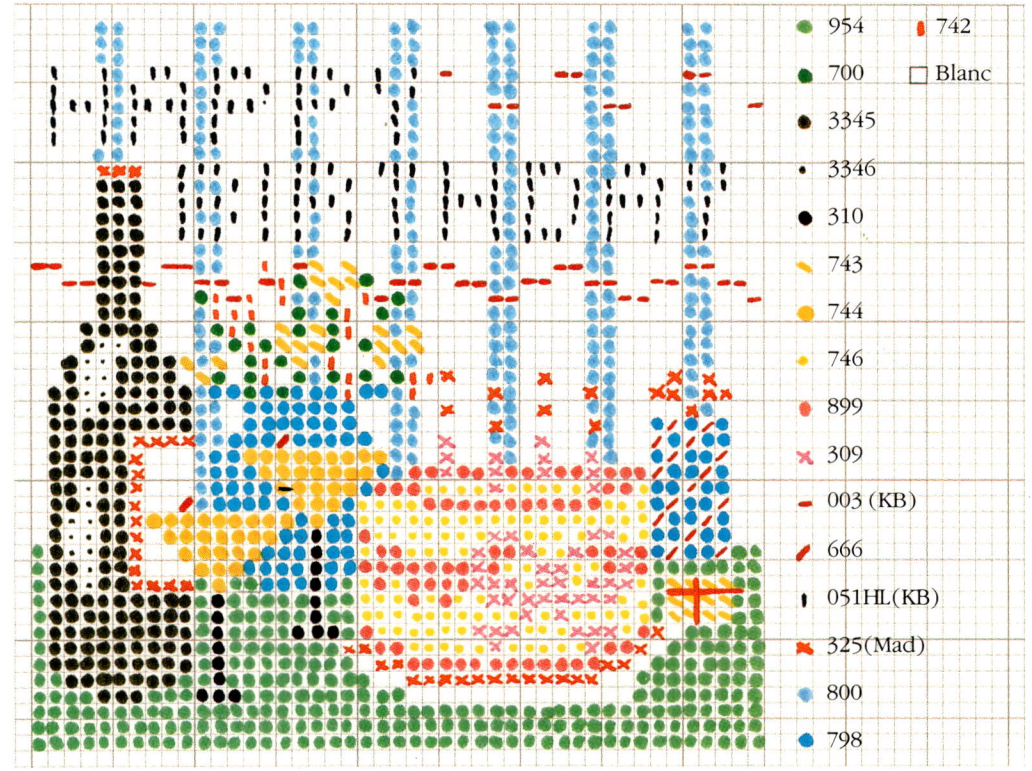

Happy Birthday and Heart Cards

NEW ARRIVAL

Congratulations in the form of a hand-stitched new-baby card will be a treasured keepsake.

NEEDLE Size 22
CANVAS 18 holes per inch (7 holes per cm)
SIZE OF CANVAS 4½ x 4½in (115 x 115mm)
SIZE OF FINISHED DESIGN 2½ x 2½in (64 x 64mm)
- Stranded cottons (floss) as listed on the chart key
- Mount card 3-fold white parchment card with 2½in (64mm) pre-cut window

1 Find the centre point on the canvas and position the design as described in Basic Techniques.
2 Count from the centre point to the top of the crib and start stitching here.
3 Work colour by colour filling in the details. Work the white background last.
4 Exchange the baby's name (up to 7 letters) for the words 'New Baby' using the alphabet on page 127 if you wish. You can of course use traditional pink or blue, or choose any other colour that you like.
5 Use 1 strand of blue 798 to backstitch the window frame. Use 1 strand of pink 335 to backstitch the outline of the crib.
6 Mount the card following the instructions in Basic Techniques. A piece of narrow ribbon tied around the fold of the card as shown makes a very pretty finishing touch.

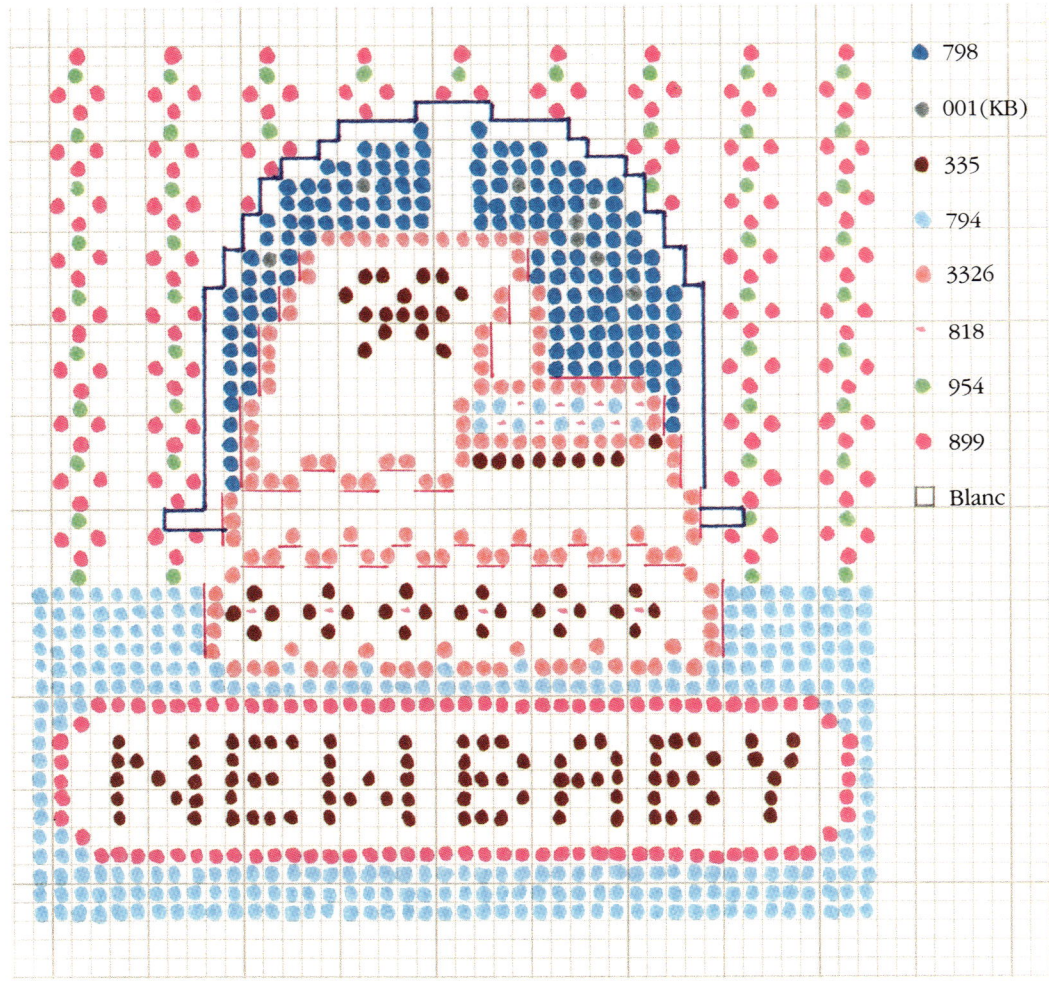

New Arrival Baby Card

DMC	COLOUR	ANCHOR
818	Very Pale Pink	48
3326	Pale Pink	25
899	Pink	52
335	Dark Pink	41
954	Green	203
798	Blue	131
794	Pale Blue	129
Blanc	White background	01

KREINIK
  BALGER Fine Braid 8:
| | Silver | 001 |

TEDDY AND BALLOONS

Personalise this charming card by including an initial from the alphabet chart.

NEEDLE Size 22
CANVAS 18 holes per inch (7 holes per cm)
SIZE OF CANVAS 5 x 5in (125 x 125mm)
SIZE OF FINISHED DESIGN 2½in (64mm) diameter
☐ Stranded cottons (floss) as listed on the chart key
☐ Mount card 3-fold card with 2½in (64mm) pre-cut round window

1   Find the centre point on the canvas and position the design as described in Basic Techniques.
2   Count the number of stitches from the centre point to the top of the teddy's head and start stitching here. Work colour by colour.
3   Choose the initial you require from the alphabet chart and work it to the left of the teddy within the square indicated on the chart. Use any colour you wish.
4   Ample stitches have been allowed for the design to fit into a 2½in (64mm) round window. If you are using a card with a larger window, add more background stitches.
5   When the design is complete, oversew the balloon strings using 1 strand of blue 798.
6   Use backstitch to outline teddy with 1 strand of brown 300.
7   Mount the card following the instructions in Basic Techniques.

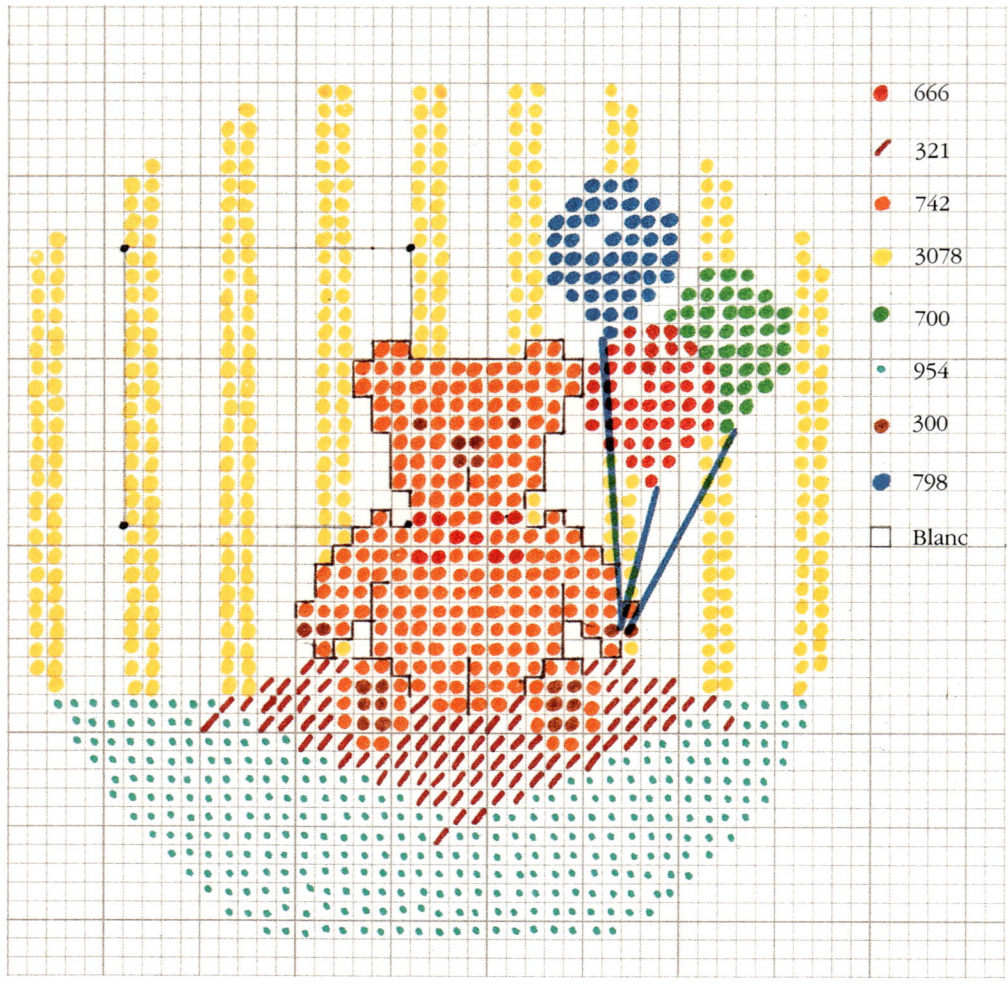

DMC	COLOUR	ANCHOR
3078	Lemon	292
798	Blue	131
666	Red	46
700	Bright Green	228
954	Green	203
321	Burgundy	47
742	Gold	303
300	Brown	352
Blanc	White	01

CHAPTER 3

CHRISTMAS

CHRISTMAS has been observed in some form since the fourth century, but the Victorians introduced many of the traditions that we now celebrate, such as the decorated Christmas tree and even the Christmas card.

The little red-breasted Robin evokes winter along with the rich greens of holly, ivy and mistletoe. Father Christmas, or Santa Claus, that wonderfully genial white-bearded, red-suited gentleman, epitomises Christmas as he fills stockings, rides sleighs and climbs down chimneys.

The hand-stitched designs in this chapter include some of these traditional themes and ensure that our messages of good will are not forgotten once Christmas is over. Commercial Christmas cards are not dated, but you can date or personalise your cards using the alphabet and numbers on Page 127. For special friends or relatives such thoughtful greetings could become an annual collection.

The smaller cards could be made into tree decorations by following the making-up instructions for the Star. All you need is a little fabric, wadding, braid and ribbon.

The many different colours and thicknesses of metallic threads are extremely useful for livening up your Christmas projects. The Star decoration with coloured metallic dots and the bright red Christmas bow will hopefully provide plenty of sparkle on the tree and last a lifetime.

Christmas Bow and Robin on a Snowy Bough

CHRISTMAS BOW

This lovely Christmas Bow can be used to trim a wreath or hung on the Christmas tree.

NEEDLE Size 22
CANVAS 18 holes per inch (7 holes per cm)
SIZE OF CANVAS 11 x 7½in (280 x 190mm)
SIZE OF FINISHED DESIGN 8 x 4¼in (203 x 108mm)
- Stranded cottons (floss) as listed on the chart key
- Wadding (Batting)
- Backing fabric: White glazed cotton 11 x 7½in (280 x 190mm)
- Red satin ribbon ½in (12mm) wide x 1⅔yd (1.5m) long

1 Find the centre point on the canvas and position the design as described in Basic Techniques.
2 Count from the centre point on the chart on pages 34-35 to the top left-hand flower and start stitching here. Working colour by colour complete the flowers and foliage.
3 Stitch the red background using 4 strands of thread and leave spaces for the metallic gold. Do not work the centre panel marked on the chart as this is left blank to make it easier to make up. Complete the design by stitching the metallic gold.
4 Block the needlepoint as described in Basic Techniques.
5 For instructions for making up the bow, see page 88, steps 4, 5 and 6.

DMC	COLOUR	ANCHOR
666	Red (6 skeins)	46
772	Pale Green	253
3347	Green	266
744	Yellow	295
Blanc	White	01
MADEIRA	Metallic gold	325

ROBIN ON A SNOWY BOUGH

This appealing winter scene can be admired all year through.

NEEDLE Size 22
CANVAS 18 holes per inch (7 holes per cm)
SIZE OF CANVAS 5½ x 5½in (140 x 140mm)
SIZE OF FINISHED DESIGN 3¼ x 3¼in (83 x 83mm)
- Stranded cottons (floss) as listed on chart key

1 Find the centre point on the canvas and position the design as described in Basic Techniques.
2 Count the number of stitches from the centre point to the top of the robin's head and start stitching here. Work colour by colour. Stitch the white areas last.
3 Oversew the robin's beak using 2 strands of brown 898. Oversew legs using 2 strands of brown 898 and his claws using 1 strand of brown 898.
4 Outline robin's eye in backstitch using 1 strand of white.
5 Use 1 strand of black 310 to make a French knot in the top right corner of the robin's eye.
6 Our picture was professionally mounted and framed.

DMC	COLOUR	ANCHOR
Blanc	White	01
310	Black	403
936	Dark Green	846
3346	Mid Green	267
794	Blue	129
415	Grey	398
898	Dark Brown	380
433	Mid Brown	358
436	Light Brown	368
666	Red	46
742	Gold	303
321	Burgundy	47

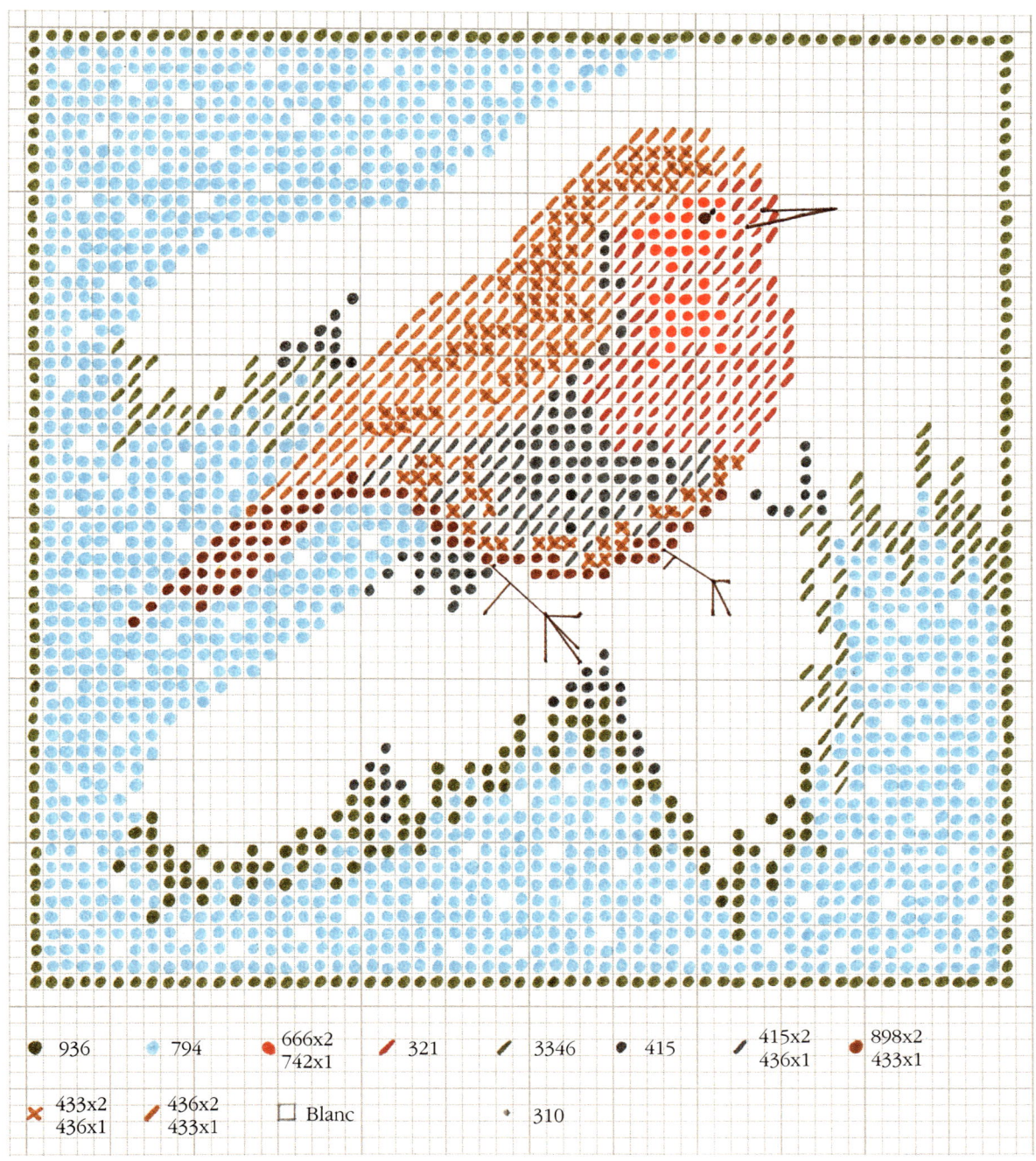

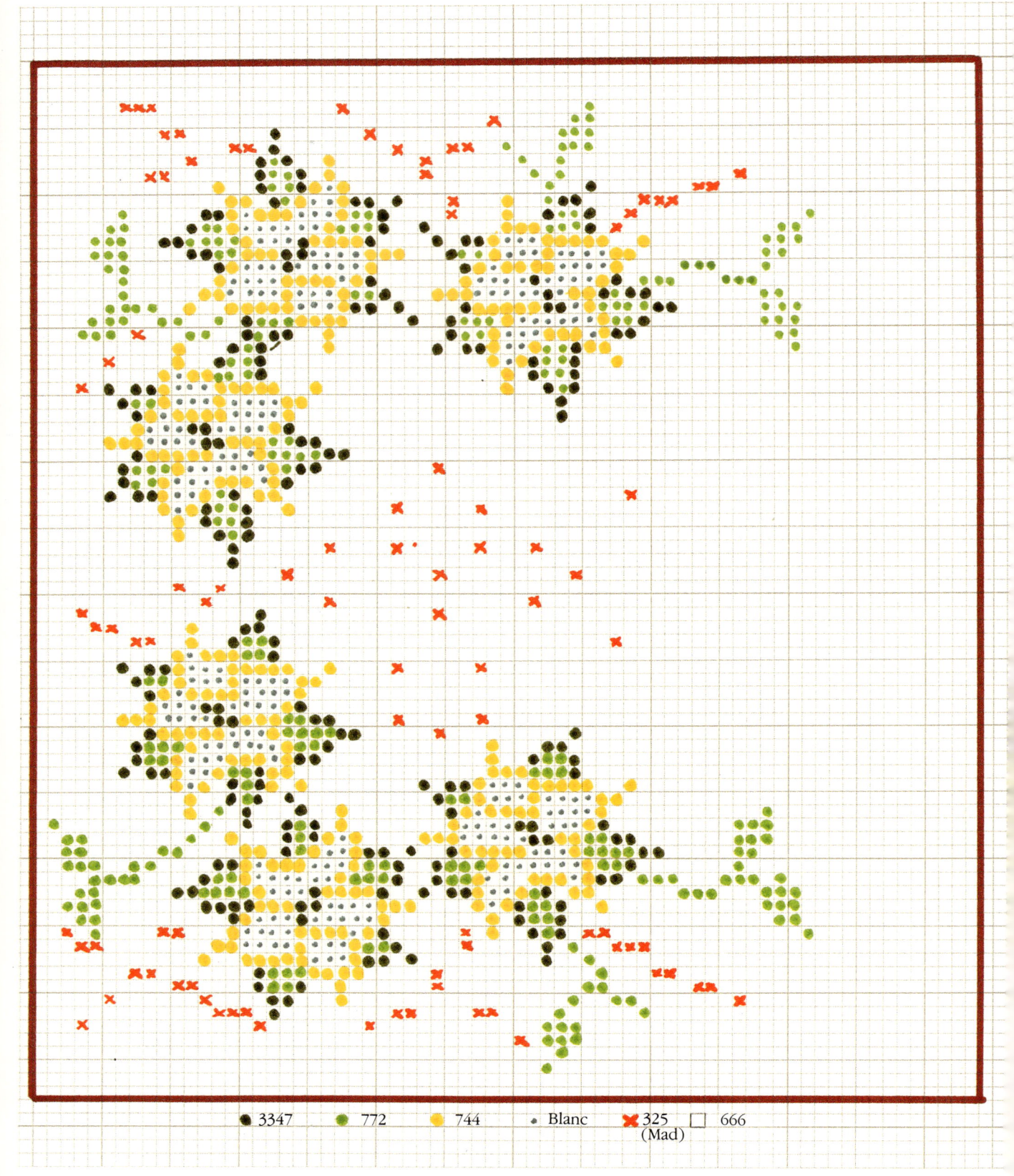

Christmas bow

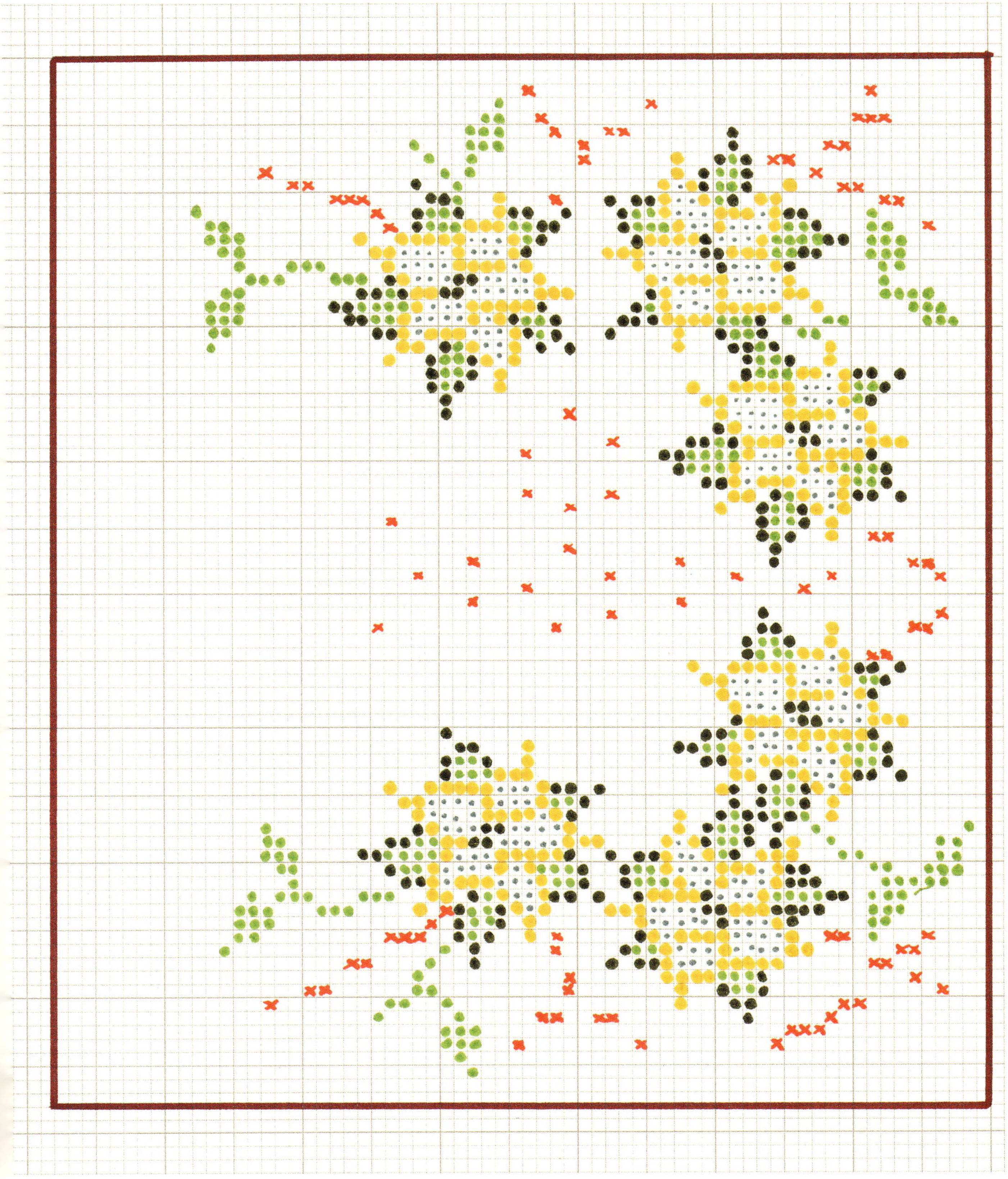

TWINKLING STAR

This sparkling decoration could be on the top of the Christmas tree for years to come.

NEEDLE Size 22
CANVAS 18 holes per inch (7 holes per cm)
SIZE OF CANVAS 10½ x 10½in (267 x 267mm)
SIZE OF FINISHED DESIGN 6½ x 6½in (165 x 165mm) at the widest point
- Stranded cottons (floss) and metallic threads as listed on the chart key
- Wadding (Batting)
- Backing fabric: Cream satin 10 x 10in (250 x 250mm)
- Gold braid for hanging

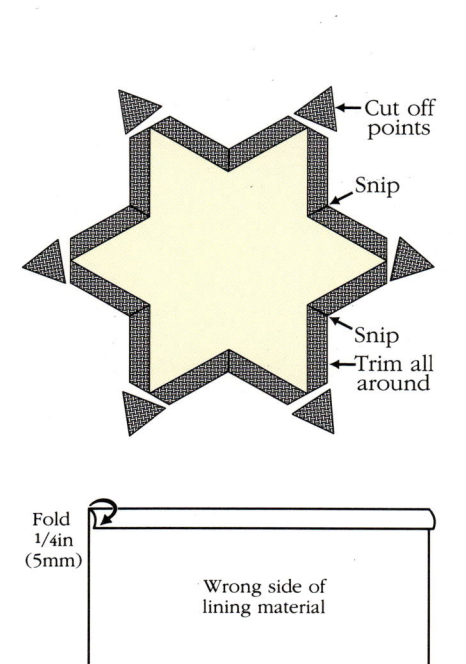

1 Find the centre point on the canvas and position the design as described in Basic Techniques.
2 Count from the centre point to the tip of the top right point and start stitching here. Complete the yellow background, leaving spaces for the metallic threads and centre gold star.
3 Work the metallic threads colour by colour and stitch the metallic gold centre star.
4 To complete the design outline the gold centre star with large single stitches using red metallic thread.
5 Block your needlework as described in Basic Techniques. Trim the canvas to ¼in (5mm) all round. Seal the canvas edges with Fray Check as close to the stitching as possible. Cut horizontally across the tip of each point as close to the stitches as possible. Snip the base of each point as close to the stitching as possible.
7 Cut the lining fabric into two. Fold back the first ¼in (5mm) on one long side of each piece and press.
8 Place needlework and one piece of backing fabric right sides together, with the folded side across the centre of the Star and pin. With the canvas side facing you, backstitch around the edge of the star as close to the needlepoint as possible.
9 Repeat with the other half of the backing fabric, making sure that the centre seams meet. Trim the backing fabric to the same size as the canvas.
10 Carefully turn inside out, gently easing out the points. Fill the points and centre with wadding. Close the centre lining seam with whipstitch or ladder stitch. Attach a length of gold braid to one of the points as a hanger.

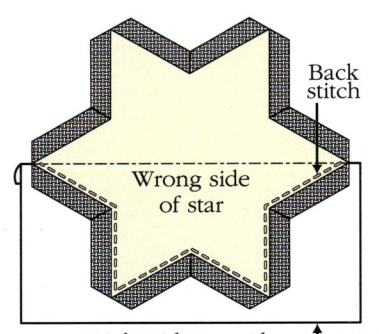

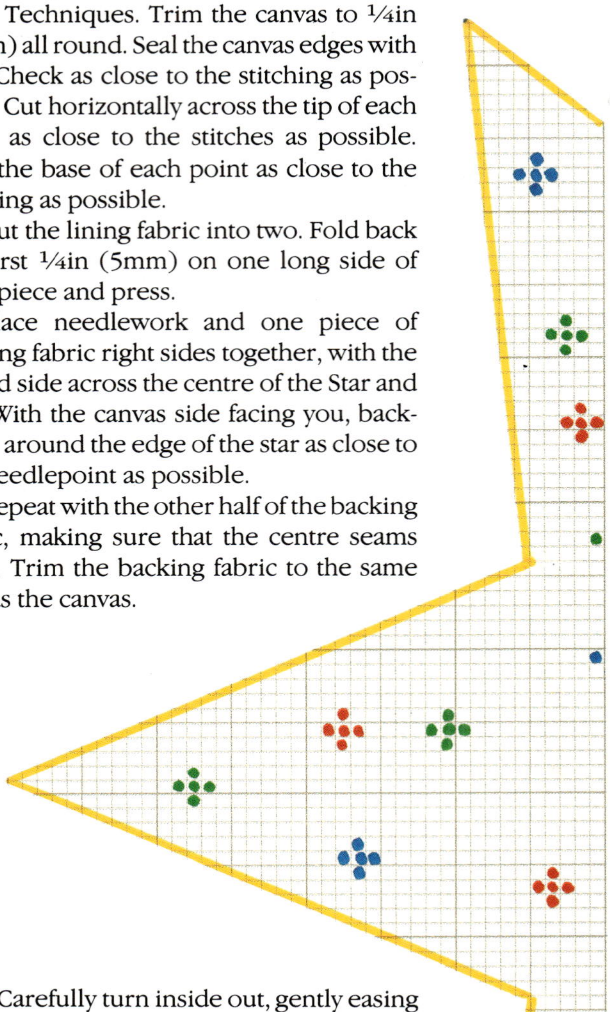

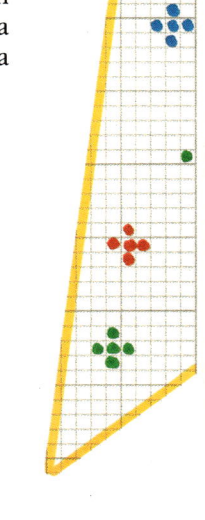

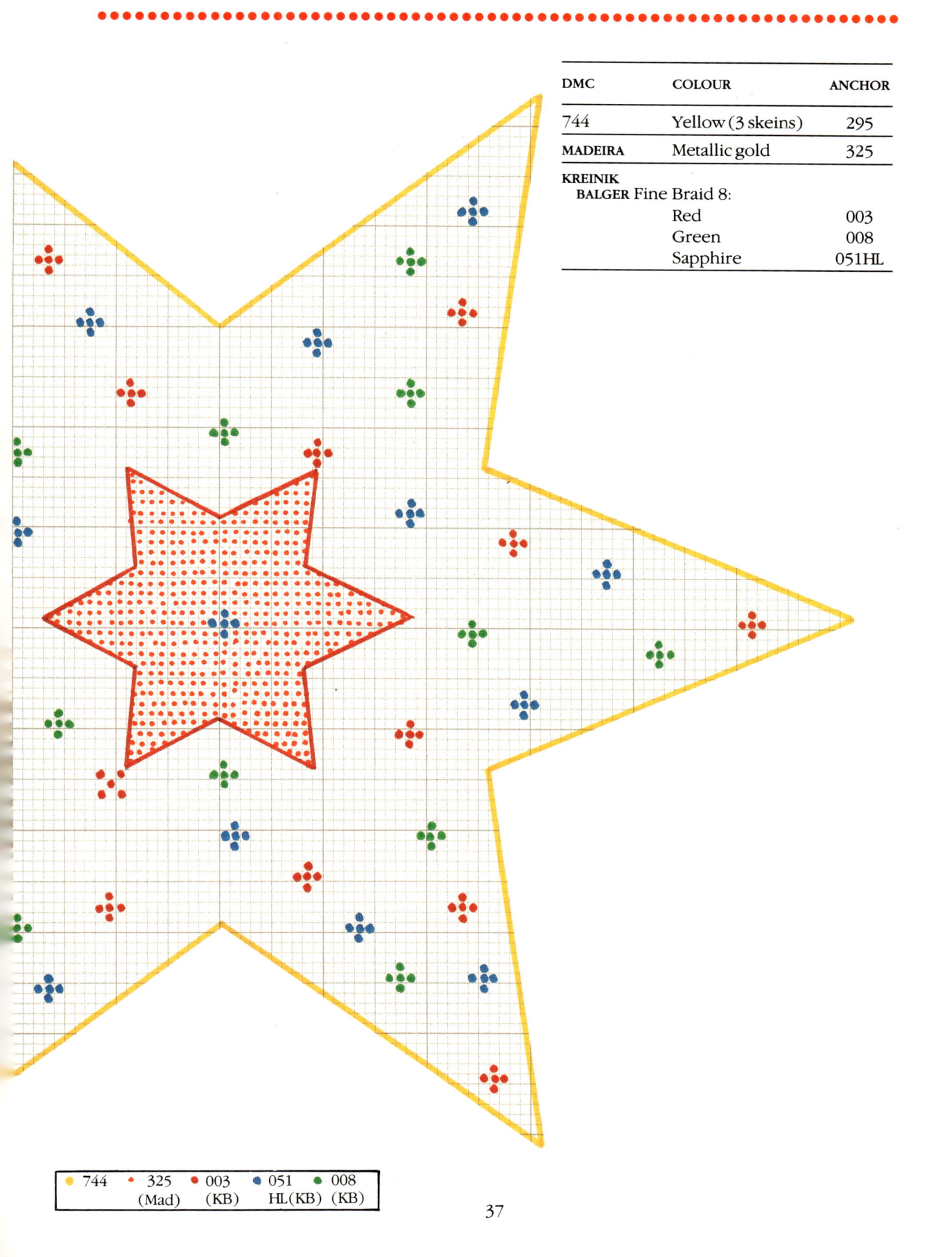

DMC	COLOUR	ANCHOR
744	Yellow (3 skeins)	295
MADEIRA	Metallic gold	325
KREINIK BALGER Fine Braid 8:		
	Red	003
	Green	008
	Sapphire	051HL

744   325 (Mad)   003 (KB)   051 HL(KB)   008 (KB)

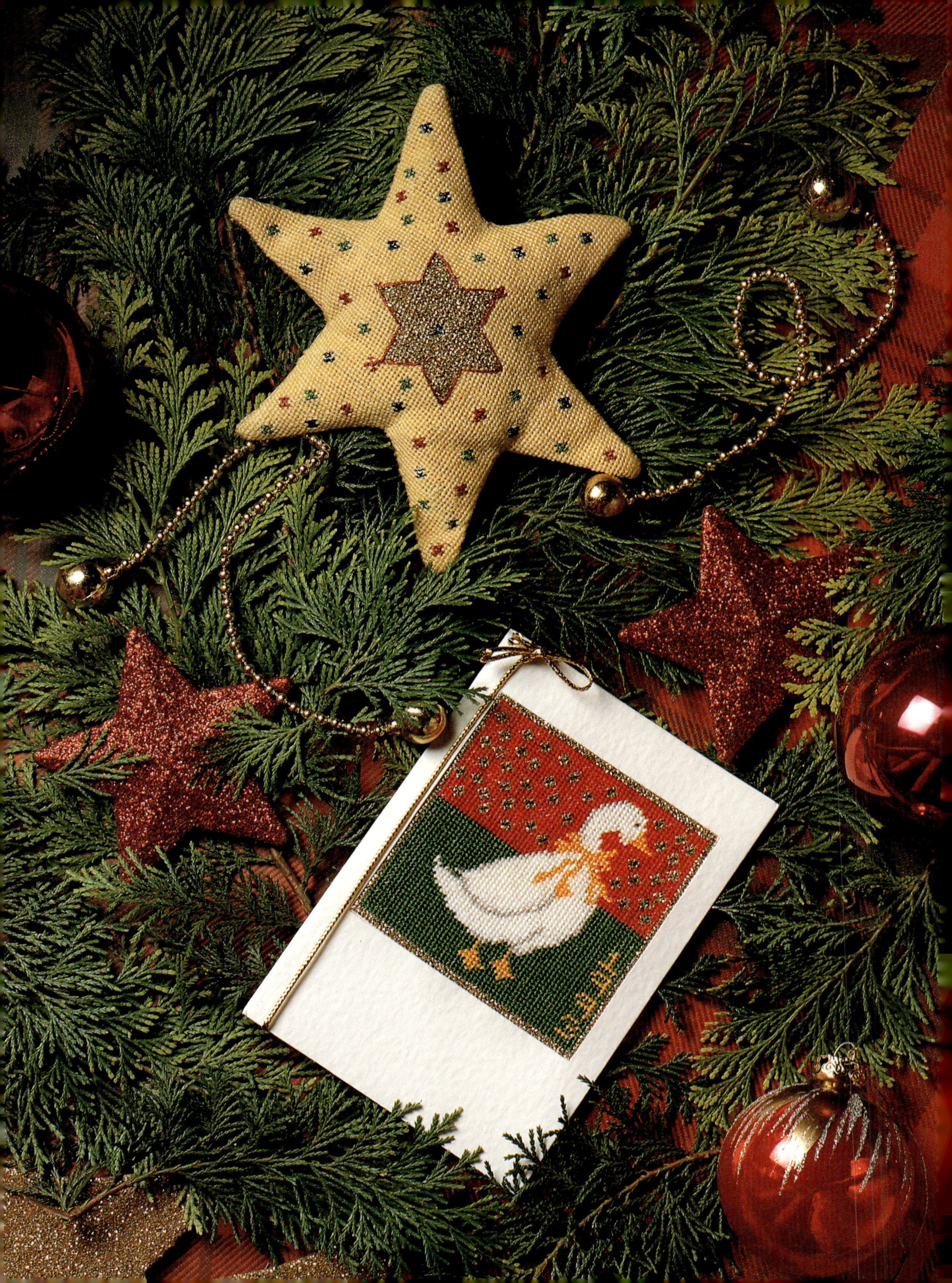

CHRISTMAS GOOSE

The rich red and green of this card conjure up the warmth of Christmas.

NEEDLE Size 22
CANVAS 18 holes per inch (7 holes per cm)
SIZE OF CANVAS 5½ x 5½in (140 x 140mm)
SIZE OF FINISHED DESIGN 3¼ x 3¼in (83 x 83mm)
- Stranded cottons (floss) and metallic threads as listed in the chart key
- Mount card 3-fold white parchment card with 3¼in (83mm) square pre-cut window
- Gold braid 12in (30cm) length

1 Find the centre point on the canvas and position the design as described in Basic Techniques.
2 Count the number of stitches from the centre point to the top of the goose's head and start stitching here. Work colour by colour. Stitch the metallic threads last.
3 Use the number chart on page 127 to work the date in gold 742 in the blank squares on the chart. Complete the background by filling in around the numbers in green 700.
4 Mount the card following the instructions in Basic Techniques. Tie a piece of gold braid in the fold of the card and make a bow at the top.

Christmas Goose Card and Christmas Star

DMC	COLOUR	ANCHOR
415	Grey	398
666	Red	46
742	Gold	303
310	Black	403
700	Green	228
Blanc	White	01
MADEIRA	Metallic Gold	325

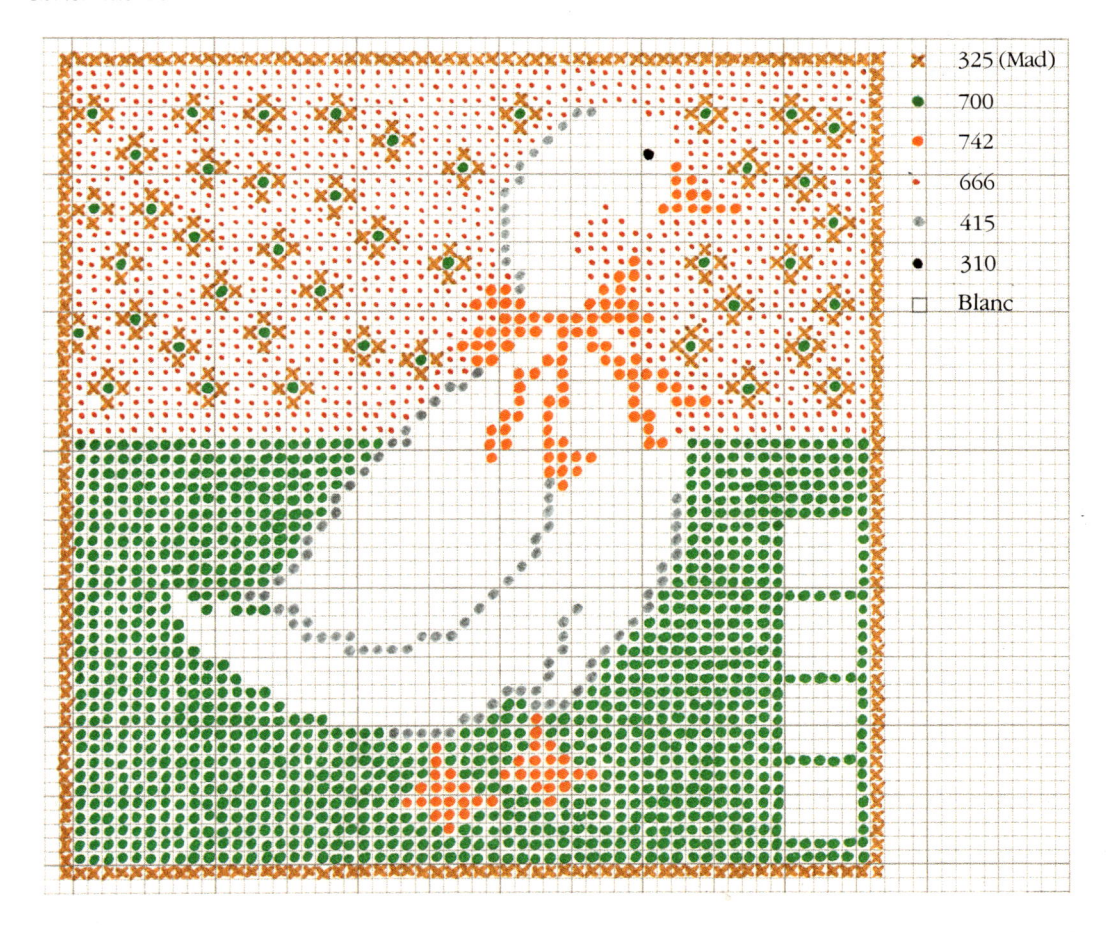

CHRISTMAS TREE

The metallic threads make this festive Christmas tree come alive.

NEEDLE Size 22
CANVAS 18 holes per inch (7 holes per cm)
SIZE OF CANVAS 4½ x 4½in (115 x 115mm)
SIZE OF FINISHED DESIGN 2½ x 2½in (64 x 64mm)
- Stranded cottons (floss) and metallic threads as listed on the chart key
- Mount card 3-fold green card with 2½in (64mm) pre-cut square window

1 Find the centre point on the canvas and position the design as described in Basic Techniques.
2 Count from the centre point to the base of the tree and start stitching here. Work colour by colour to complete the tree. Leave the metallic threads until last.
3 Sew the presents and the tree holder before working the border, then fill in the background.
4 To complete the design 'wrap' the parcels by oversewing with either 1 strand of cotton thread or metallic gold thread as shown. To make the star, oversew a 6-pointed cross in metallic gold thread. A silver thread zigzags across the tree six times in a random fashion.
5 Mount the card following the instructions in Basic Techniques.

DMC	COLOUR	ANCHOR
Blanc	White	01
3345	Dark Green	268
700	Bright Green	228
954	Light Green	203
666	Red	46
310	Black	403
798	Blue	131
300	Brown	352
743	Yellow	305
MADEIRA	Metallic Gold	325
KREINIK BALGER Fine Braid 8:		
	Red	003
	Silver	001

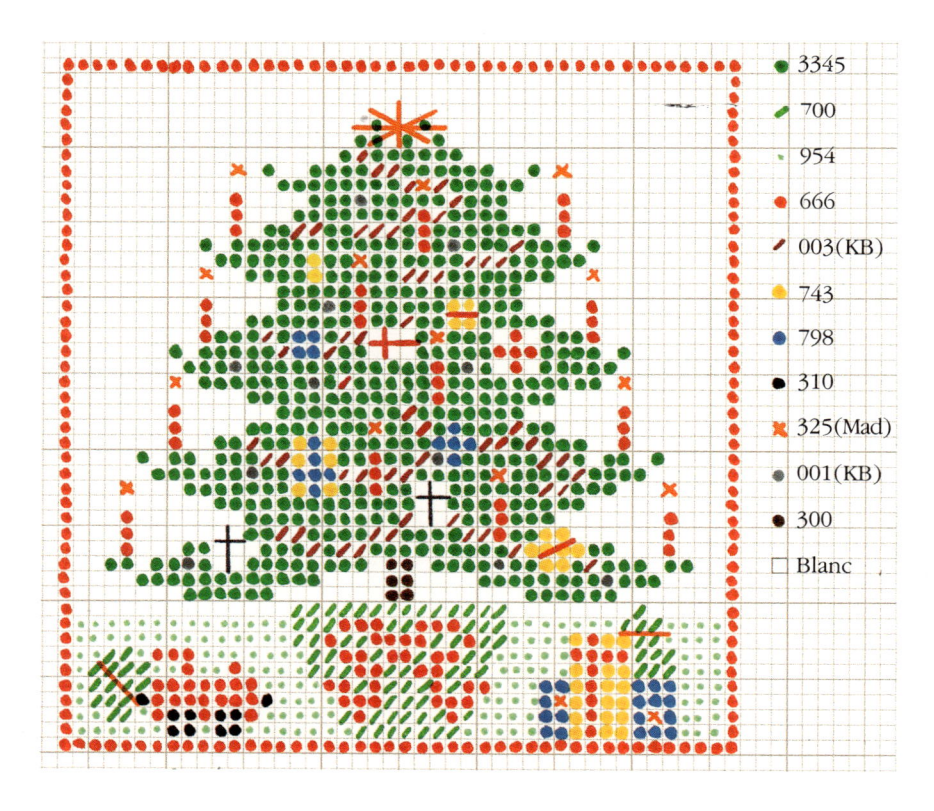

CHRISTMAS CAT

This cat looks particularly comfortable on his rich red cushion.

NEEDLE Size 22
CANVAS 18 holes per inch (7 holes per cm)
SIZE OF CANVAS 5 x 5in (125 x 125mm)
SIZE OF FINISHED DESIGN 2½in (64mm) diameter
- Stranded cottons (floss) and metallic thread as listed on the chart key
- Mount card 3-fold gold foil card with 2½in (64mm) pre-cut round window

1 Find the centre point on the canvas and position the design as described in Basic Techniques.
2 Count the number of stitches from the centre point to the dark brown line in the centre of the cat's body and start stitching here. Work colour by colour. Work the metallic gold threads last.
3 Oversew the cat's whiskers and outline the cat's body in backstitch with 1 strand of brown 300.
4 Ample stitches have been allowed for the design to fit into a 2½in (64mm)-diameter window. For a larger opening simply add more background stitches.
5 Mount the card following the instructions in Basic Techniques.

DMC	COLOUR	ANCHOR
745	Cream	300
676	Ochre	891
729	Dark Ochre	890
300	Brown	352
310	Black	403
666	Red	46
321	Burgundy	47
Blanc	White	01
700	Green	228
MADEIRA	Metallic Gold	325

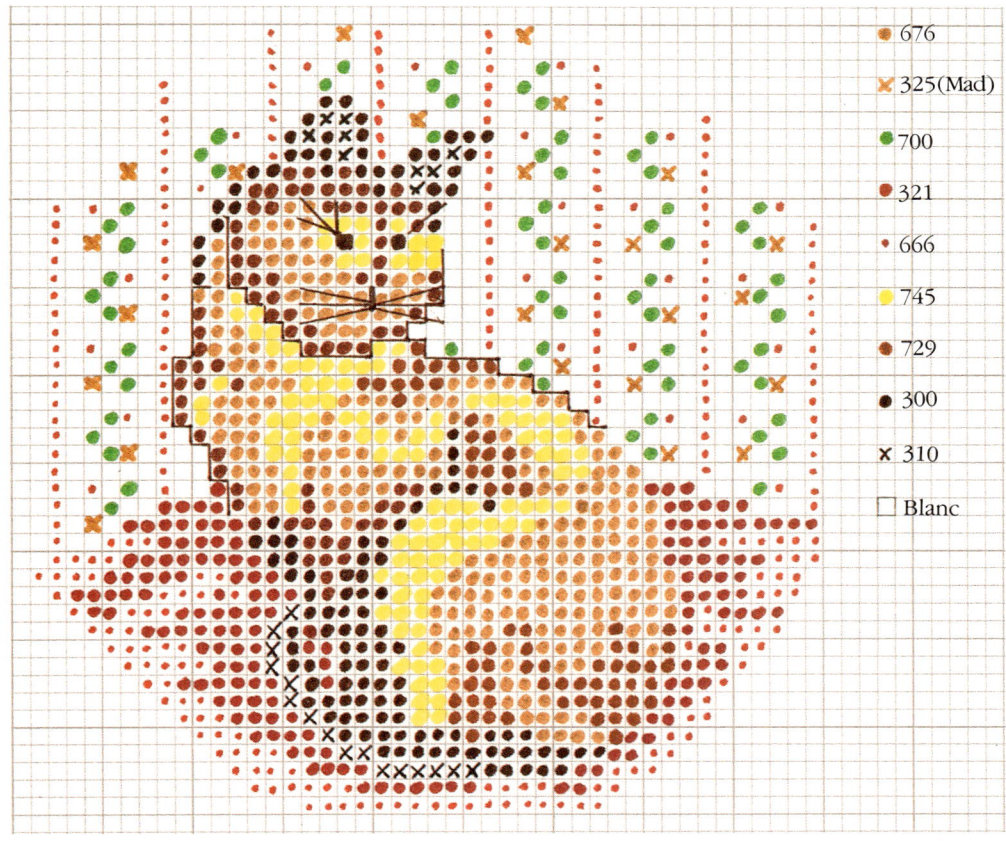

(Overleaf) Christmas Tree, Christmas Wreath, Father Christmas and Christmas Cat Cards

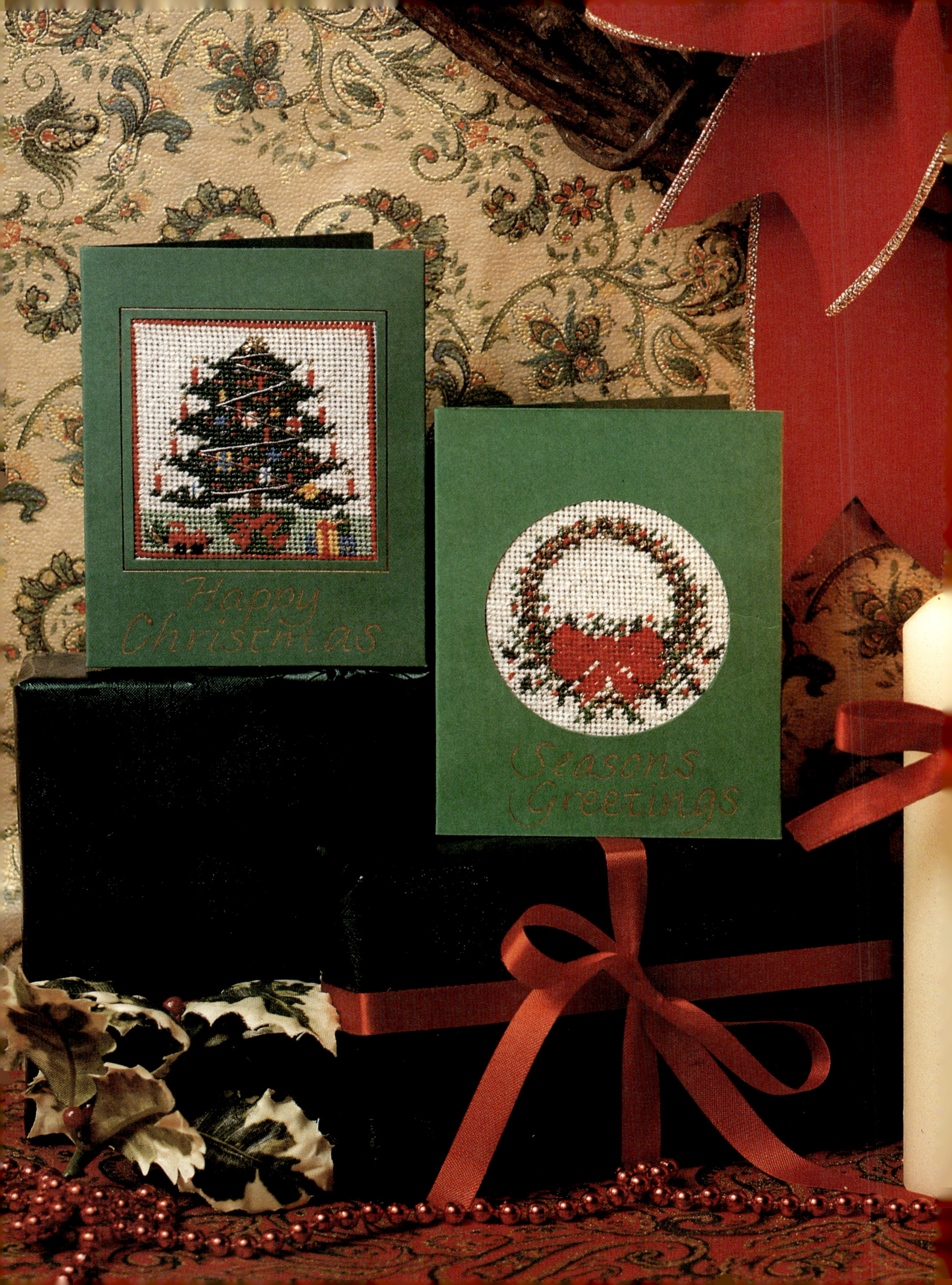
Happy Christmas
Seasons Greetings

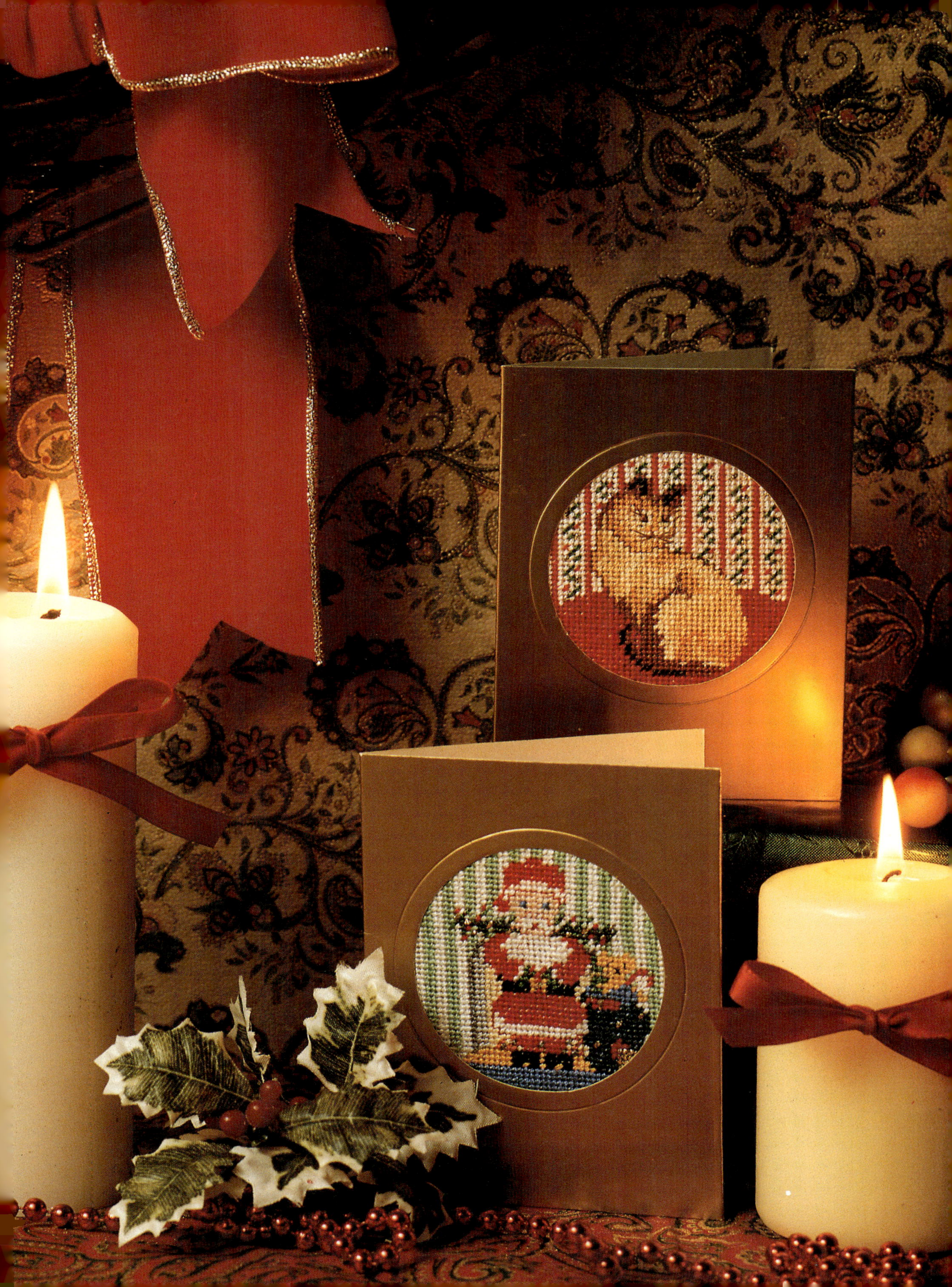

HO! HO! HO!

A jolly Father Christmas stands in front of the fireplace with his sack of presents.

NEEDLE Size 22
CANVAS 18 holes per inch (7 holes per cm)
SIZE OF CANVAS 5x 5in (125 x 125mm)
SIZE OF FINISHED DESIGN 2½in (64mm) diameter
- Stranded cottons (floss) and metallic threads as listed on the chart key
- Mount card 3-fold gold foil card with 2½in (64mm) round window

1 Find the centre point on the canvas and position the design as described in Basic Techniques.
2 Count from the centre point to the top of Father Christmas's hat and start stitching here.
3 Working colour by colour, except gold thread. Complete all details before working background wallpaper. Work details in metallic thread last.
4 Complete the design by backstitching the outlines of the hat and fur at the base of the jacket using 1 strand of red 666. Use 1 strand of pink 335 to backstitch his moustache. The eyes are made by a crossed stitch of blue 798. Use 1 strand of black 310 to oversew across the teddy's nose and a single vertical line for each eye.
5 Mount the card following the instructions in Basic Techniques. Ample stitches have been allowed for the design to fit into a 2½in (64mm) window. For a larger opening simply add more background stitches.

DMC	COLOUR	ANCHOR
954	Light Green	203
700	Bright Green	228
3345	Dark Green	268
666	Red	46
745	Cream	300
742	Gold	303
754	Flesh Pink	6
336	Dark Blue	148
798	Blue	131
310	Black	403
317	Dark Grey	400
415	Grey	398
720	Orange	326
Blanc	White	01
335	Pink	41
MADEIRA	Metallic Gold	325

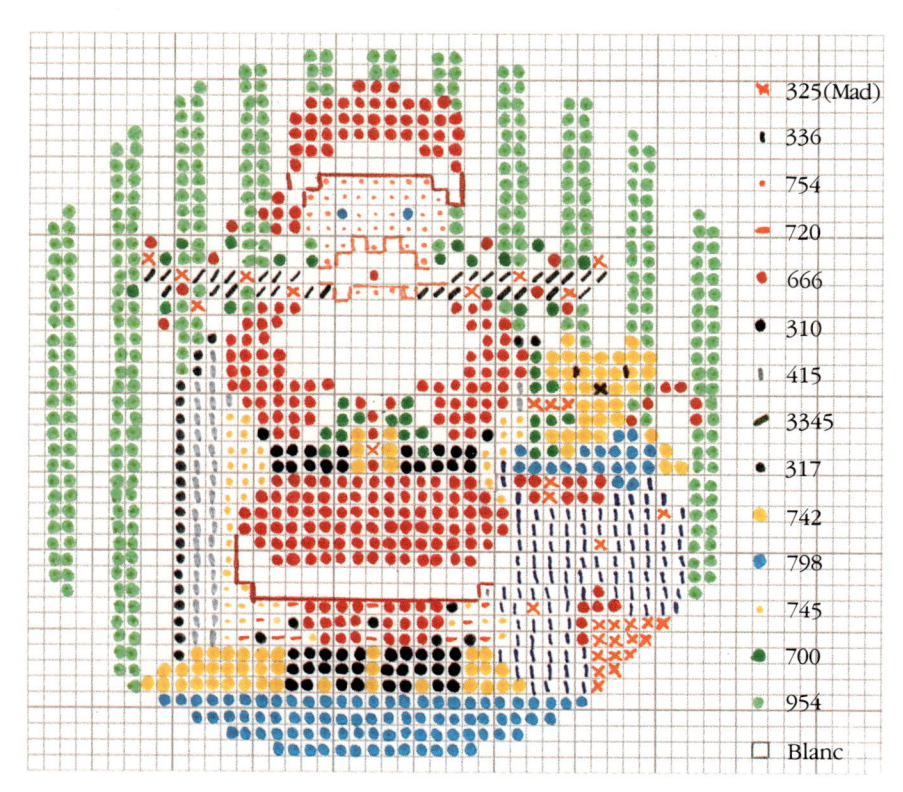

CHRISTMAS WREATH

One of the most traditional decorations is the holly wreath with a big red bow.

NEEDLE Size 22
CANVAS 18 holes per inch (7 holes per cm)
SIZE OF CANVAS 5 x 5in (125 x 125mm)
SIZE OF FINISHED DESIGN 2½ x 2½in (64mm x 64mm) approx.
- Stranded cottons (floss) and metallic threads as listed on the chart key
- Mount card 3-fold green card with pre-cut round window, 2½in (64mm) diameter. A strong coloured card brings out the design.

1 Find the centre point on the canvas and position the design as described in Basic Techniques.
2 Count from the centre point to the top of the bow's knot and start stitching here. Complete the bow before working the wreath. Work colour by colour, leaving the metallic thread until last.
3 Complete by working the white background. Ample stitches have been allowed for the design to fit into a 2½in (64mm) window. For a larger opening simply add more background stitches.
4 Mount the card following the instructions in Basic Techniques.

Note: When mounting a light coloured stitched background on a strong coloured card, the card may deaden the piece. Place a small piece of white paper behind the piece before gluing the flap.

DMC	COLOUR	ANCHOR
700	Bright Green	228
3345	Dark Green	268
666	Red	46
816	Deep Red	20
3032	Beige	392
3031	Brown	380
Blanc	White	01
MADEIRA	Metallic Gold	325

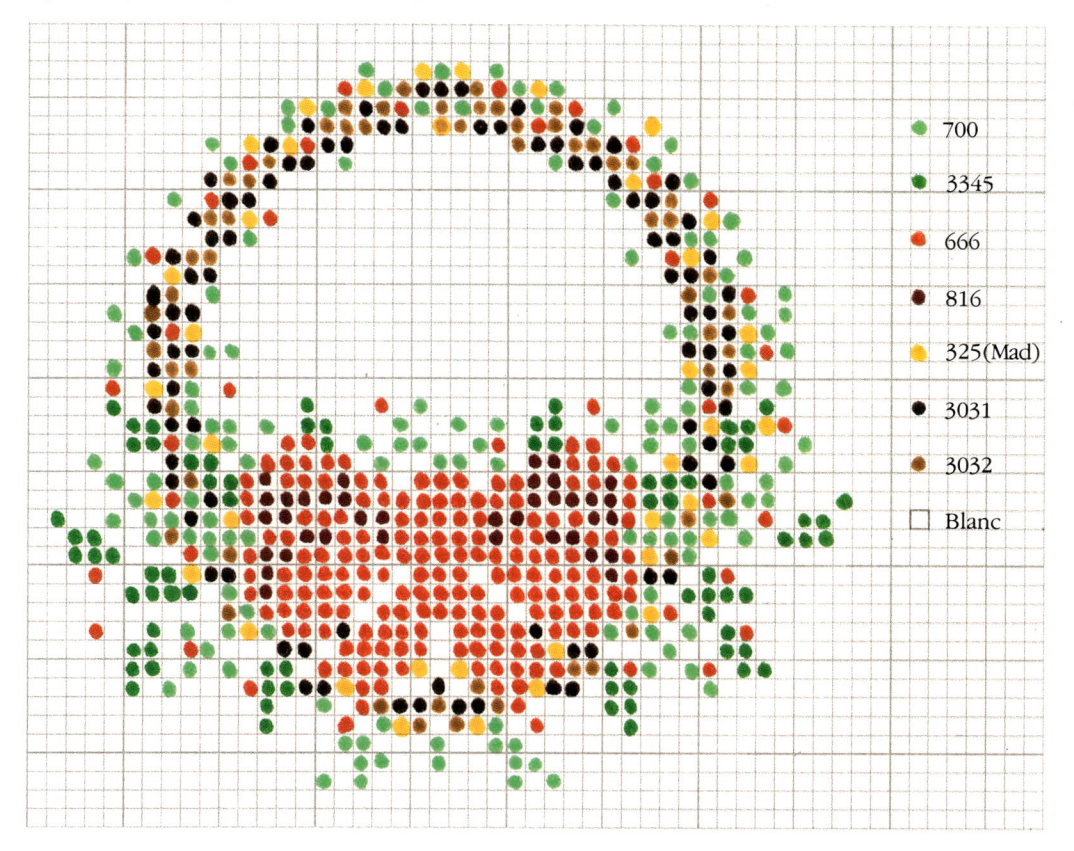

CHAPTER 4

THE NURSERY

THUMBELINA Designs really began in our children's clothes shop. A small needlepoint picture on the wall with a name, birthdate and a row of cars and trains attracted a lot of attention and admiration. Many of our customers and friends were looking for unusual birth and christening gifts and a personalised picture was the perfect solution. Children love to see things with their names on them. They also like strong colours and simple, bold motifs that they can relate to. Emma, Judy's daughter, loves rabbits, which made a good starting point for 'her' sampler featured in this chapter. These simple motifs make it easy for the novice designer to create panels of nursery toys and familiar objects.

The wonderful thing about stitching a picture for the nursery is that it gives pleasure not only to the child but to the whole family – hopefully for a lifetime and more. Such individual pieces are treasured now and will become collectible 'samplers' in years to come.

Both the Teddy Bears' Picnic and the Rabbits projects would be ideal for an 'unknown' new baby as they are suitable for either a boy or girl and can be worked to the point of placing the name and date, which can be completed after the baby is born.

The Rabbits and the Cars are particularly good for adapting to individual requirements. A selection of charts on pages 52–55 enables you to choose a complete strip or to piece together different motifs to create your own unique designs.

Several strips can be incorporated into a design and the colours can be changed. If you're working the sampler for an older child, why not let them help choose the motifs and colours? Use the alphabet and number charts on page 48 to plot the child's name and birthdate on graph paper. If the name is short, you can add simple motifs such as flowers or trees.

The alphabet cushion, worked on 14-hole canvas with 6 strands of cotton (floss), combines several small designs. Hidden in the pictures is at least one object for each letter of the alphabet. You could add more or different motifs.

Benjamin Sampler and Jennifer's Fairy

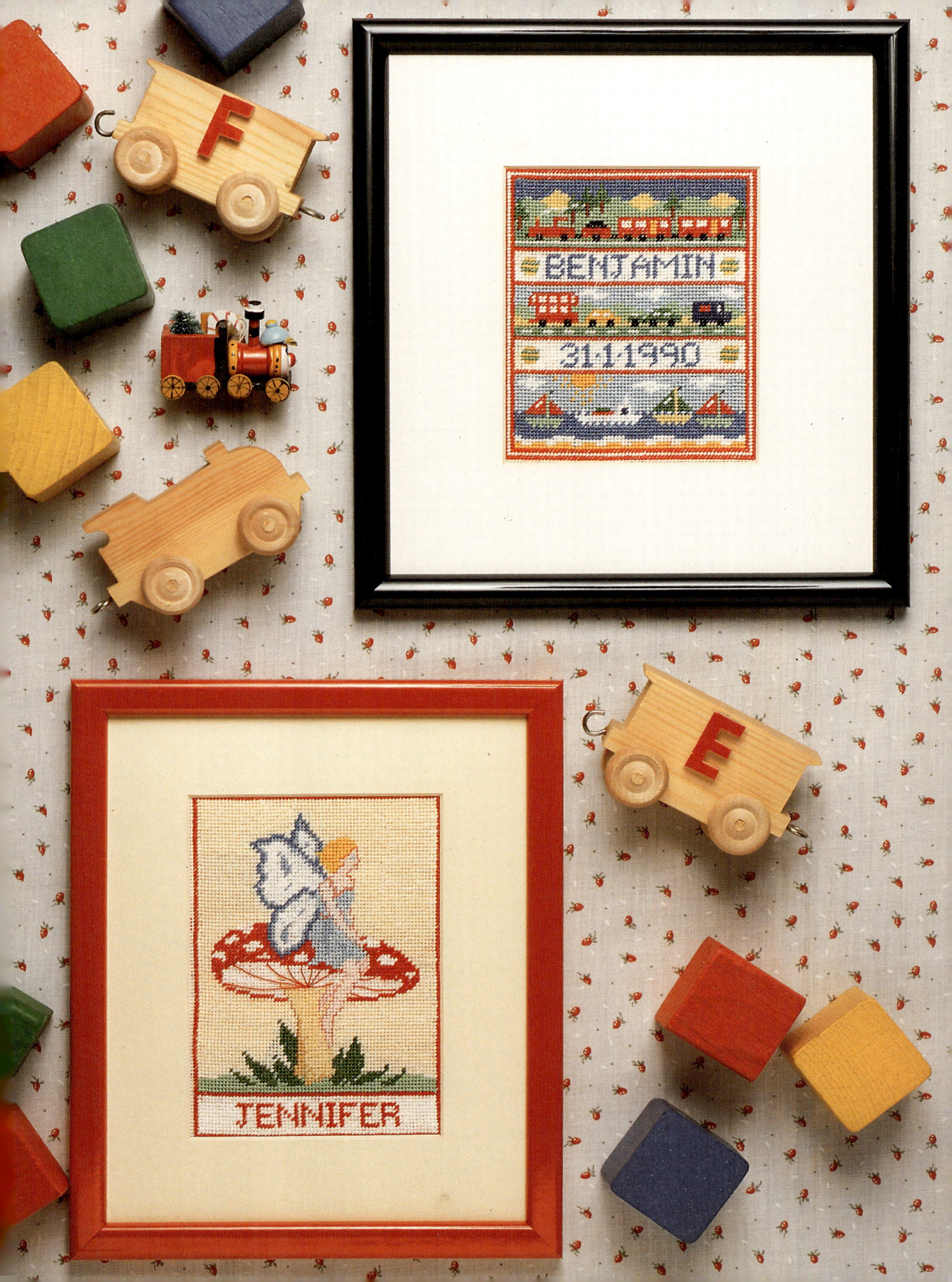
BENJAMIN
31.1.1990
JENNIFER

JENNIFER'S FAIRY

Thumbelina's trademark, an enchanting fairy sitting on a plump toadstool, was the inspiration for this design.

NEEDLE Size 22
CANVAS 18 holes per inch (7 holes per cm)
SIZE OF CANVAS 7 x 9in (180 x 230mm)
SIZE OF FINISHED DESIGN 3⅞ x 5½in (100 x 140mm)
☐ Stranded cottons (floss) as listed on the chart key
Note This design is suitable for any name up to 10 letters.

1 Find the centre point on the canvas and position the design as described in Basic Techniques.
2 Count from the centre point to the top of the fairy's dress and start stitching here. Complete the fairy colour by colour before moving on to the toadstool and background details.
3 To complete the picture, outline all the pink areas using backstitch and 1 strand of dark pink 899. Create the eye with 1 strand of pale blue 800. The left side of the toadstool has a line of backstitch of 1 strand of dark gold 782 to emphasise it. With 1 strand of red 666 oversew with one long stitch the underside segments of the toadstool as indicated. Stitch the red border including the area for the name.
4 Use the alphabet to work the required name (see Graphing Letters and Numbers on page 14).
5 Work the background area around the name.
6 This project was professionally mounted and framed using a cream mount and an inexpensive red lacquered frame to echo the border.

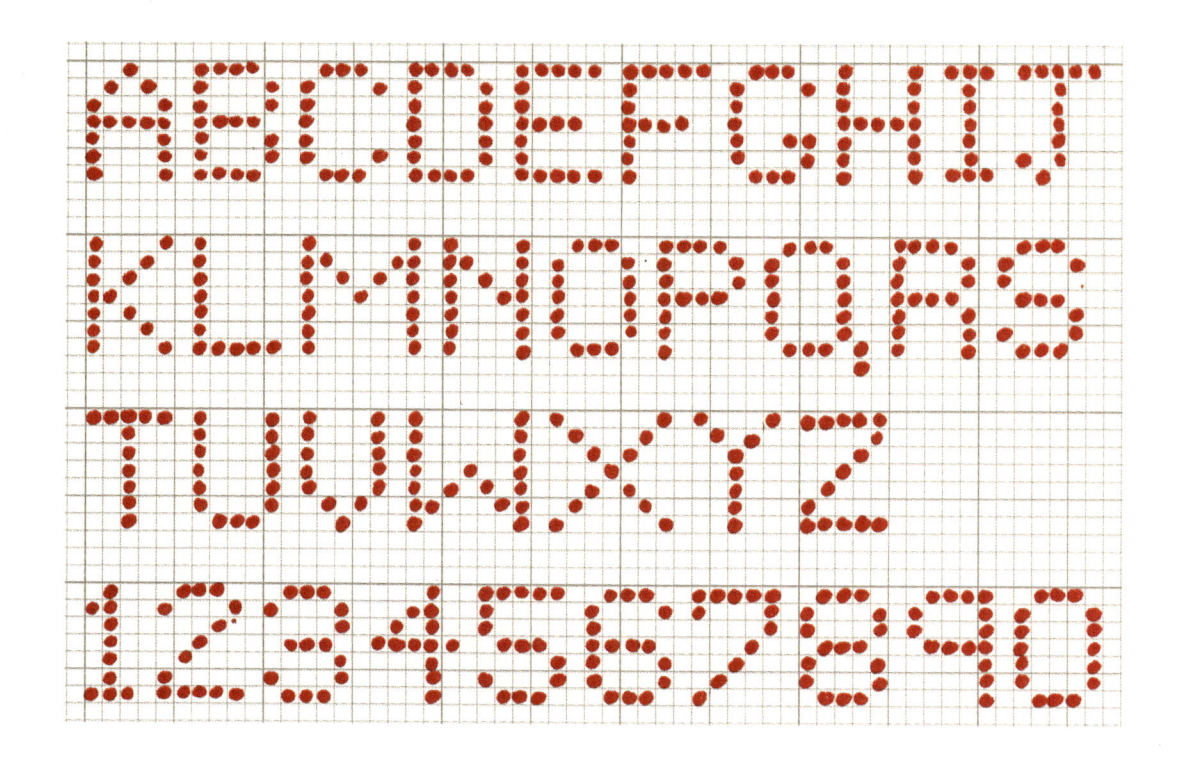

DMC	COLOUR	ANCHOR
666	Bright Red	46
954	Light Green	203
700	Bright Green	228
800	Pale Blue	128
794	Blue	129
798	Dark Blue	131
743	Yellow	305
742	Dark Yellow	303
899	Dark Pink	52
818	Pale Pink	48
3326	Pink	25
745	Dark Cream	300
676	Ochre	891
782	Dark Gold	307
Blanc	White	01
746	Cream background (2 skeins)	386

| • 666 | • 954 | • 700 | • 676 | – 745 | ╱ 794 | • 800 | • 798 |
| • 899 | • 818 | ╱ 818x2
3326x1 | • 743x2
742x1 | • 746 | ☐ Blanc | | |

EMMA'S SWANS AND RABBITS

This delightful sampler uses interchangeable strip charts to create a treasured gift for a new baby.

NEEDLE Size 22
CANVAS 18 holes per inch (7 holes per cm)
SIZE OF CANVAS 8 x 8¾in (200 x 220mm)
SIZE OF FINISHED DESIGN 4 x 4¾in (102 x 120mm)
☐ Stranded cottons (floss) as listed on chart key
Note This design is suitable for any name up to 10 letters.

1. Find the centre point on the canvas and position the design as described in Basic Techniques.
2. Count from the centre point to the lower border the middle strip and start stitching here. Complete the middle strip following the chart.
3. Stitch the other strips of the design.
4. Use the alphabet on page 48 to make up the required name (see Graphing Letters and Numbers on page 14). For longer names, omit one or both flower motifs.
5. Repeat this process to position the date of birth, allowing three stitch spaces between the day, month and year.
6. Stitch the outer border.
7. Oversew the rabbit's whiskers using 1 strand of white as shown in the photograph.
8. Use 1 strand of black 310 and make French knots for the swans' eyes as shown.
9. Mount and frame as preferred. This project was framed professionally.

DMC	COLOUR	ANCHOR
798	Blue	131
800	Pale Blue	128
954	Pale Green	203
912	Green	205
3078	Lemon	292
744	Yellow	295
335	Pink	41
818	Pale Pink	48
310	Black	403
Blanc	White	01

We used Pink 335 for the name and date. You can use any colour you choose.

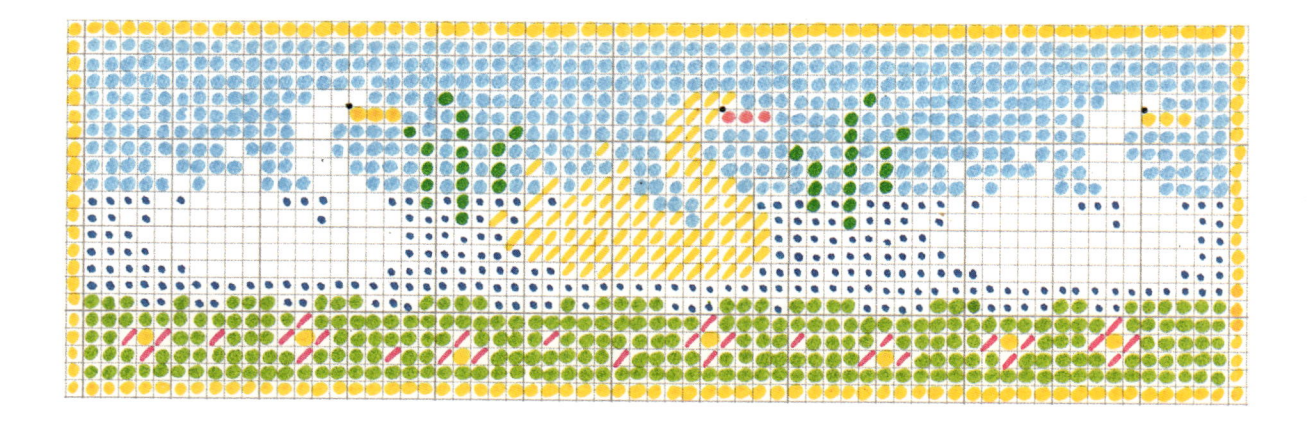

Emma's Swan and Rabbit Sampler

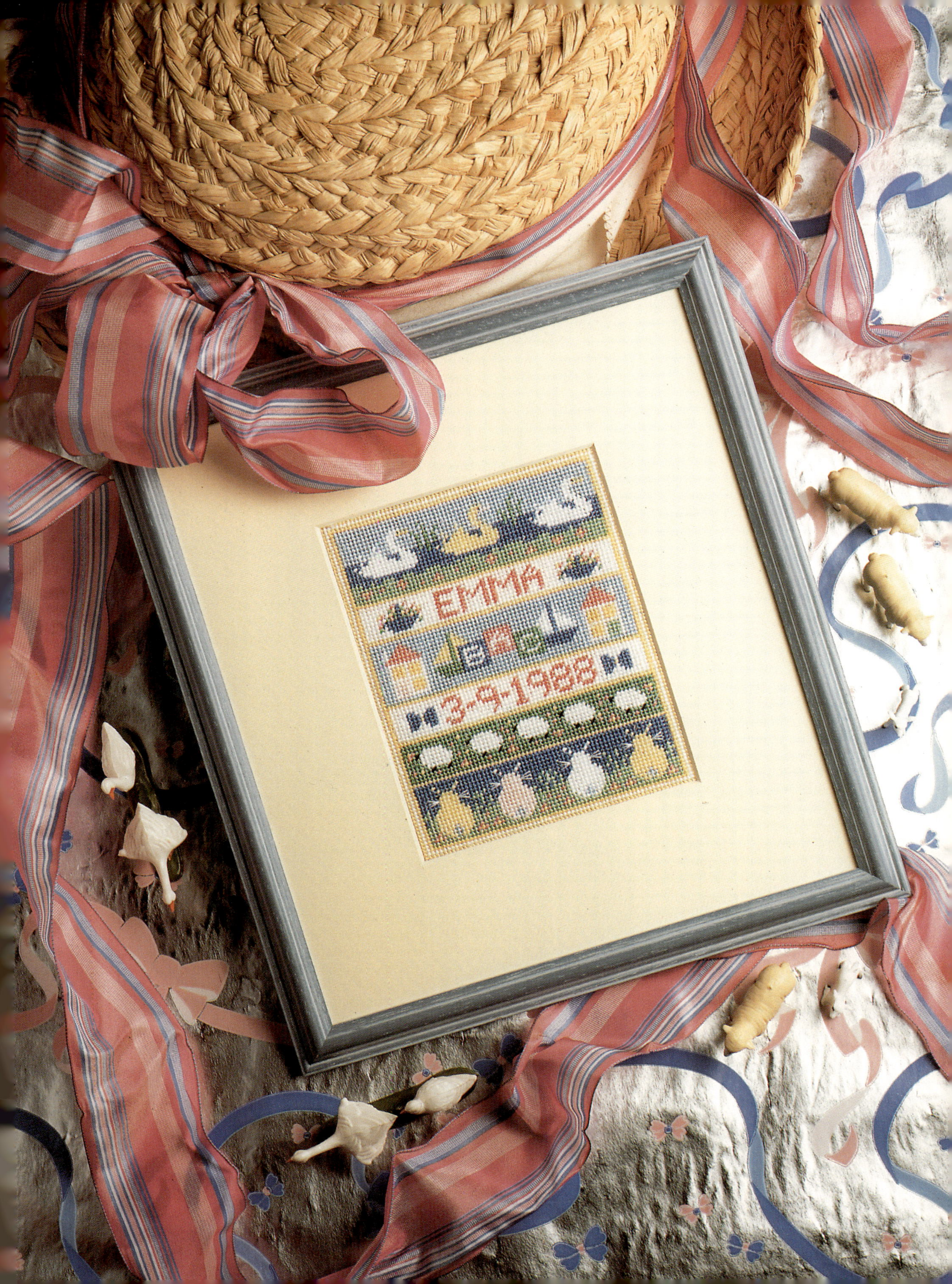
EMMA
3-9-1988

| 744 | / 3078 | • 798 | • 800 | • 818 | / 335 | • 912 | • 954 | • 310 | ☐ Blanc |

DOOR PLAQUE

You can use any of the strip charts in this chapter, or create your own, to make a delightful plaque to hang on the door of a child's room.

FINISHED DESIGN 4⅝ x 2¼in (120 x 60mm)

1 The door plaque pictured on page 1 is made using the strip chart of a train from Benjamin's Sampler on page 54. Use a piece of 14-hole canvas 7 x 4½in (175 x 115mm) and follow the instructions for 'Benjamin'. If your child has a long name, omit the word 'Room'.

2 Block your work as described in Basic Techniques. Cut a piece of fabric 7 x 4½in (175 x 115mm). Place right sides together and using backstitch, sew three sides of the door plaque, leaving the short side open. Clip the corners. Turn inside out and stitch the open side. Gently press flat. Centre a small curtain ring on the fabric and sew it in position as a hanger.

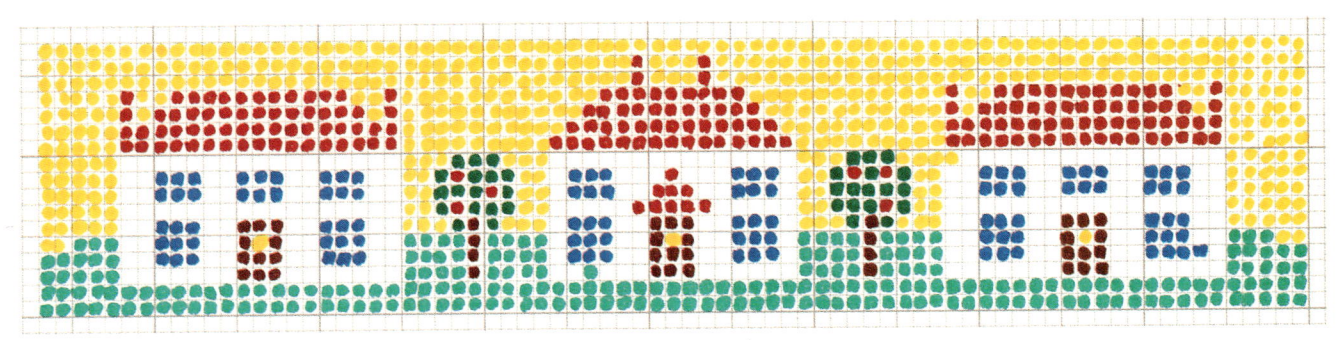

• 666	• 742	• 800	• 798	• 912	• 700	• 954	• 820	╱ 744	• 310
✗ 300	□ Blanc								

BENJAMIN'S SAMPLER

The primary colours and familiar motifs of this personalised sampler, pictured on pages 2 and 47, make it perfect for a child's room.

NEEDLE Size 22
CANVAS 18 holes per inch (7 holes per cm)
SIZE OF CANVAS 8 x 8¾in (200 x 220mm)
SIZE OF FINISHED DESIGN 4 x 4¾in (102 x 120mm)
☐ Stranded cottons (floss) as listed on the chart key
Note This design is suitable for any name up to 10 letters.

1 Find the centre point on the canvas and position the design as described in Basic Techniques.
2 Count from the centre point to the lower border of the middle strip and start stitching here. Complete the middle strip, following the chart.
3 Stitch the other strips of the design.
4 Use the alphabet on page 48 to make up the required name (see Graphing Letters and Numbers on page 14). For longer names, you could omit the ball.
5 Repeat this process to position the date of birth, allowing three stitch spaces between the day, month and year.
6 Stitch the outer border.
7 Mount and frame as preferred. This project was framed professionally in a lacquered wooden frame.

DMC	COLOUR	ANCHOR
798	Blue	131
666	Red	46
954	Light Green	203
700	Bright Green	228
912	Mid Green	205
744	Yellow	295
800	Pale Blue	128
820	Navy	134
742	Gold	303
300	Brown	352
310	Black	403
Blanc	White	01

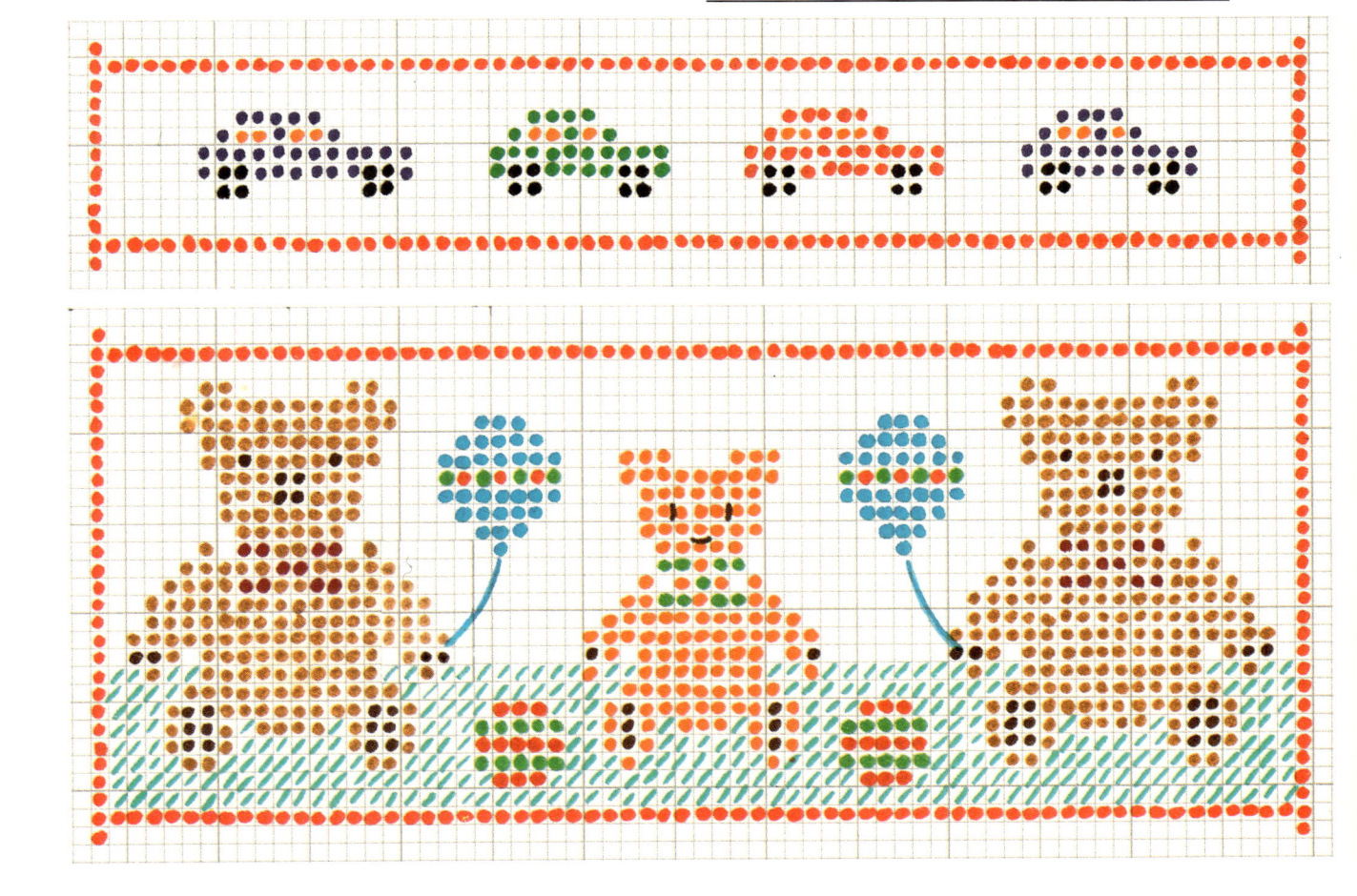

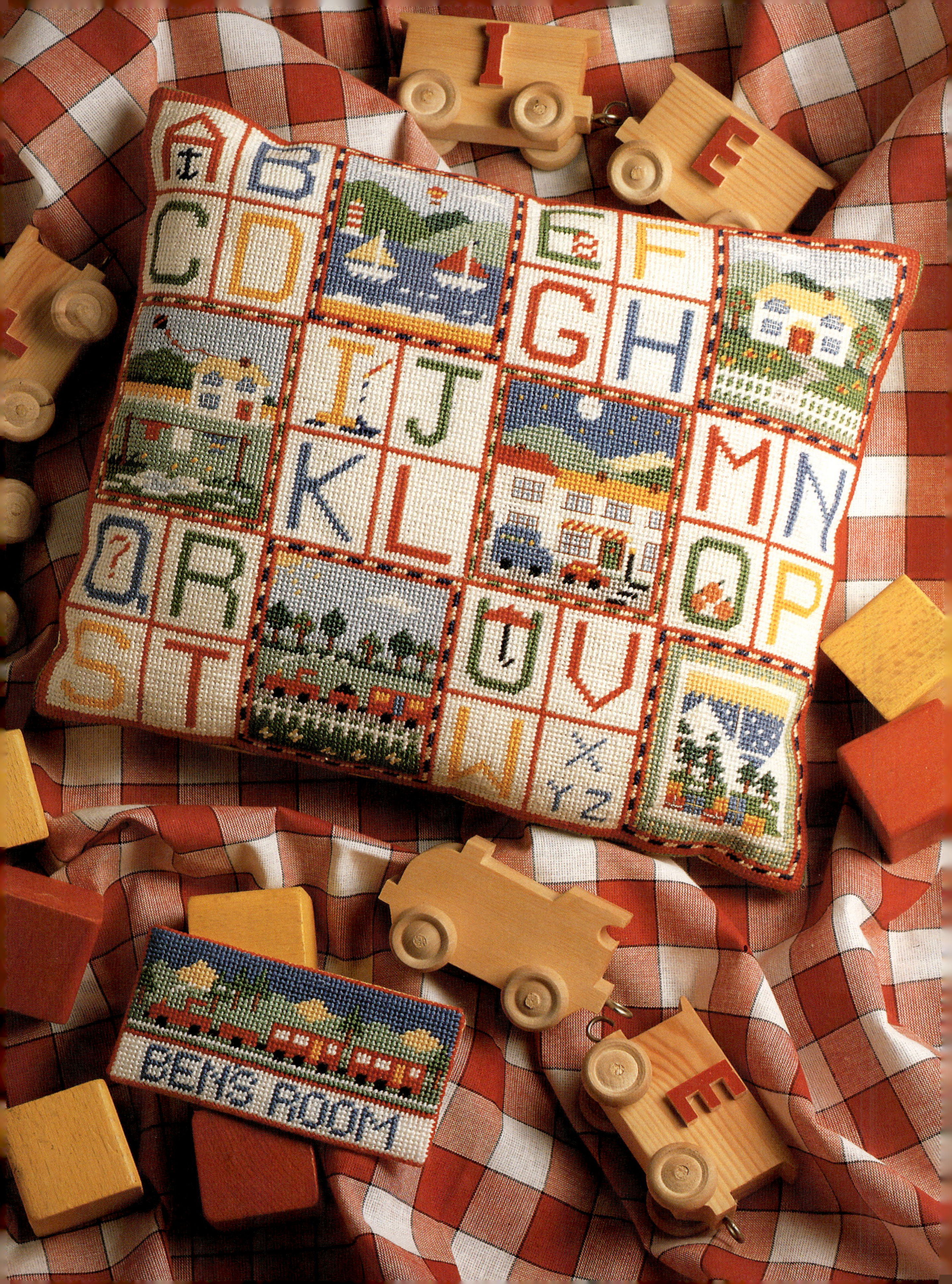
BENS ROOM

ALPHABET CUSHION

This striking cushion is a patchwork of letter squares and pictorial scenes. To puzzle and delight your child there is at least one object for every letter of the alphabet somewhere on the cushion. We have listed them all here.

A	anchor, apple	O	oranges
B	balloon	P	path, presents, puddle
C	car, chimney, clouds, coal	Q	question mark
D	door	R	road and roof
E	eight, engine	S	sea, sails, sand, sky, stars
F	fence, flowers		
G	gate, garden	T	train, tree
H	house, hill	U	umbrella
I	ink	V	van
J	jumper	W	window, washing line, wheels
K	kite, knocker		
L	lighthouse, letters	X	Xmas presents
M	moon, mountains	Y	yacht
N	number	Z	zebra crossing

NEEDLE Size 20
CANVAS 14 holes to the inch (5½ holes per cm)
SIZE OF CANVAS 18 x 16in (460 x 405mm)
SIZE OF FINISHED CANVAS 12 x 10in (305 x 255mm)
☐ Stranded cottons (floss) as listed in the chart key
☐ Backing fabric 18 x 16in (460 x 405mm)
☐ Cushion pad

1 Find the centre point on the canvas and position the design as described in Basic Techniques.
2 Use 6 strands of thread. Split the threads first and then re-combine them to help stop them from twisting as you stitch.
3 Choose the square of design with which you wish to start. Count the number of stitches from the centre point to the bottom right-hand corner of the square and start stitching here. Work colour by colour. Leave the white background until last in order to keep the work clean.
4 To complete the design oversew the cottage windows using 1 strand of white. The window panes on the row of houses are oversewn using 1 strand of brown 300. To 'tie' the parcels, oversew in long stitch. Use 1 strand each of red 666 and metallic gold 325. To create the washing line use 1 strand of brown 300 to link the posts. The kite's tail is made of 1 strand of red 666 sewn in a zigzag of long stitches. To make the stars oversew 2 strands of gold 742 in a cross stitch.
5 Block your needlework as described in Basic Techniques.
6 To make up the cushion, place the blocked needlepoint and backing fabric together right sides facing and stitch around three sides as close to the stitches as possible. Trim the edges and mitre the corners.
7 Turn inside out and press gently with a steam iron. Insert the cushion pad. Hand stitch the open edge.

DMC	COLOUR	ANCHOR
800	Pale Blue (3 skeins)	128
954	Light Green (3 skeins)	203
319	Dark Green	212
700	Bright Green (4 skeins)	228
798	Blue (3 skeins)	131
300	Brown	352
744	Yellow (2 skeins)	295
742	Gold (2 skeins)	303
970	Orange	316
820	Navy	134
317	Grey	400
310	Black	403
666	Red (5 skeins)	46
Blanc	White (11 skeins)	01
MADEIRA	Metallic Gold	325

Alphabet Cushion and Door Plaque

666	700	800	820	310	317	798	954	300	744	742	970	319	Blanc

58

Alphabet cushion left side

666	700	800	820	310	317	798	954	300	744	742	970	319	Blanc
●	●	●	●	●	●	●	●	●	●	●	／	／	□

Alphabet cushion right side

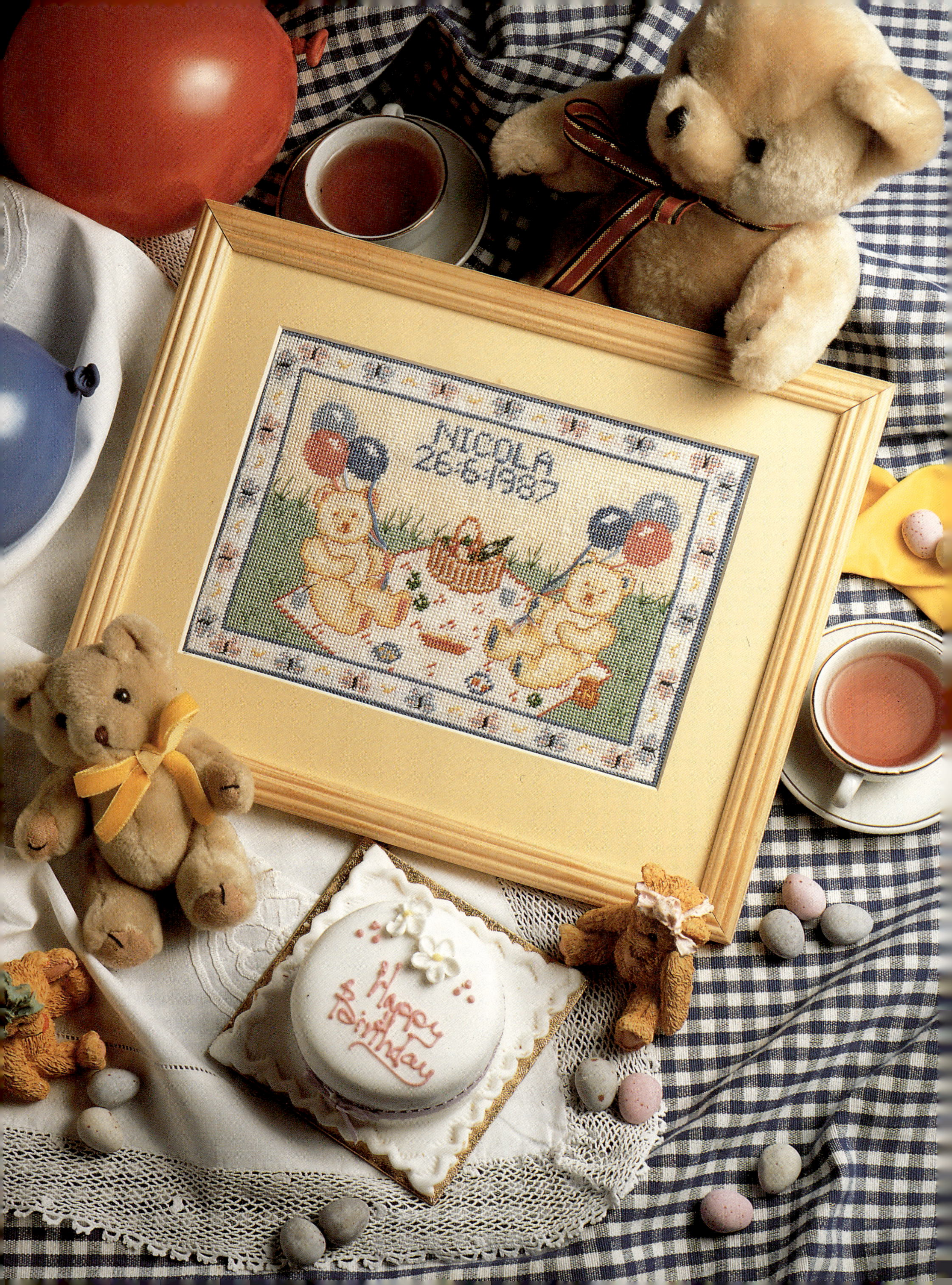
NICOLA
26·6·1987
Happy Birthday

Teddy Bear's Picnic

The Teddy Bear's Picnic nursery sampler can be personalised with up to 12 letters or worked as a nursery picture without any lettering as shown on the chart on pages 64–65.

NEEDLE Size 22
CANVAS 18 holes to the inch (7 holes per cm)
SIZE OF CANVAS 9 x 12in (230 x 305mm)
SIZE OF FINISHED CANVAS 7⅝ x 5½in (195 x 140mm)
□ Stranded cottons (floss) as listed on the chart key

1 Find the centre point on the canvas and position the design as described in Basic Techniques.
2 Count from the centre point to the base of the picnic basket and start stitching here. Work colour by colour, stitching the bears and background details except for the cream area for the name and date.
3 Stitch the inner border.
4 Use the alphabet on page 29 or 48 to work the required name and date of birth (see Graphing Letters and Numbers on page 14).
5 Stitch the background around the name and date.
6 Stitch the outer border and the butterflies before filling in with white.
7 To complete the design use backstitch to outline the bears and make the mouths with 1 strand of brown 301. Work an 'H' on the honey jar by oversewing with three strands of yellow 743. Work the grass by oversewing with long stitches using 1 strand of green 700. The balloon strings are oversewn with 3 strands of the matching colour as shown. The butterflies' antennae are oversewn with 1 strand of dark blue 336.
8 This picture was professionally mounted and framed using a cream mount and simple pine frame.

DMC	COLOUR	ANCHOR
794	Pale Blue	129
336	Dark Blue	148
798	Blue	131
743	Yellow	305
745	Dark Cream	300
746	Cream (2 skeins)	386
335	Pink	41
309	Dark Pink	39
3326	Pale Pink	25
720	Orange	326
301	Brown	349
739	Beige	942
3345	Dark Green	268
954	Light Green	203
700	Bright Green	228
912	Green	205
Blanc	White (2 skeins)	01

Teddy Bear's Picnic

Blanc 954 912 700 743 745 746 309 335 798

| 794 | 336 | 3326 | 301 | 3345 | 739 | 720 |

Teddy Bear's Picnic

CHAPTER 5

VICTORIAN TREASURES

INSPIRATION for these projects has come from the wealth of designs created for everyday objects in the Victorian period. If you enjoy browsing in antique and bric-a-brac shops, you'll find the selecting of ideas becomes as much fun as working on the projects. Look out for embroidered linens, hand-painted china, old greetings cards, Victorian paper scraps used to decorate screens and trinket boxes, and decorative ceramic tiles.

The large Poppy design is based on an unusual double tile bought in an antique market years ago. The original design has been strengthened by changing some of the colours. A vast range of colours is available in stranded cottons (floss) and the subtleties of shading can be put to good effect in petals and leaves.

The Art Nouveau style of the late nineteenth century, particularly appealing because of its flowing, curving lines, is the period from which the Canterbury Bell design originates. These flowers are highly stylised and do not need to be too detailed, as they rely on the fluidity of the outline and flat areas of colour. Cotton perlé (pearl cotton) is excellent here for defining leaves and stems. The inexperienced needleworker will appreciate the simplicity of this art-nouveau design.

Victorians were great romantics and their sentimental paintings of cottages and gardens are a good source of inspiration. Simple stitches used randomly in different floral colours among shades of green can create quite realistic gardens, like the one surrounding the little Thatched Cottage.

The Pansy and Red Campion miniature pictures were adapted from lovely late-Victorian greetings cards. Sprigs of flowers and foliage, often romantically arranged around a country scene, can be used for a variety of projects, either as a border to a larger piece, as we have done for Home Sweet Home, for decorative box lids or just as miniature pictures. Silk cigarette cards and turn-of-the century postcards are also good sources for motifs.

The vibrant colours of the butterflies on the Needlecase and Pincushion contrast with the black background and the butterflies appear to fly off the surface.

Canterbury Bells Tile and Thatched Cottage

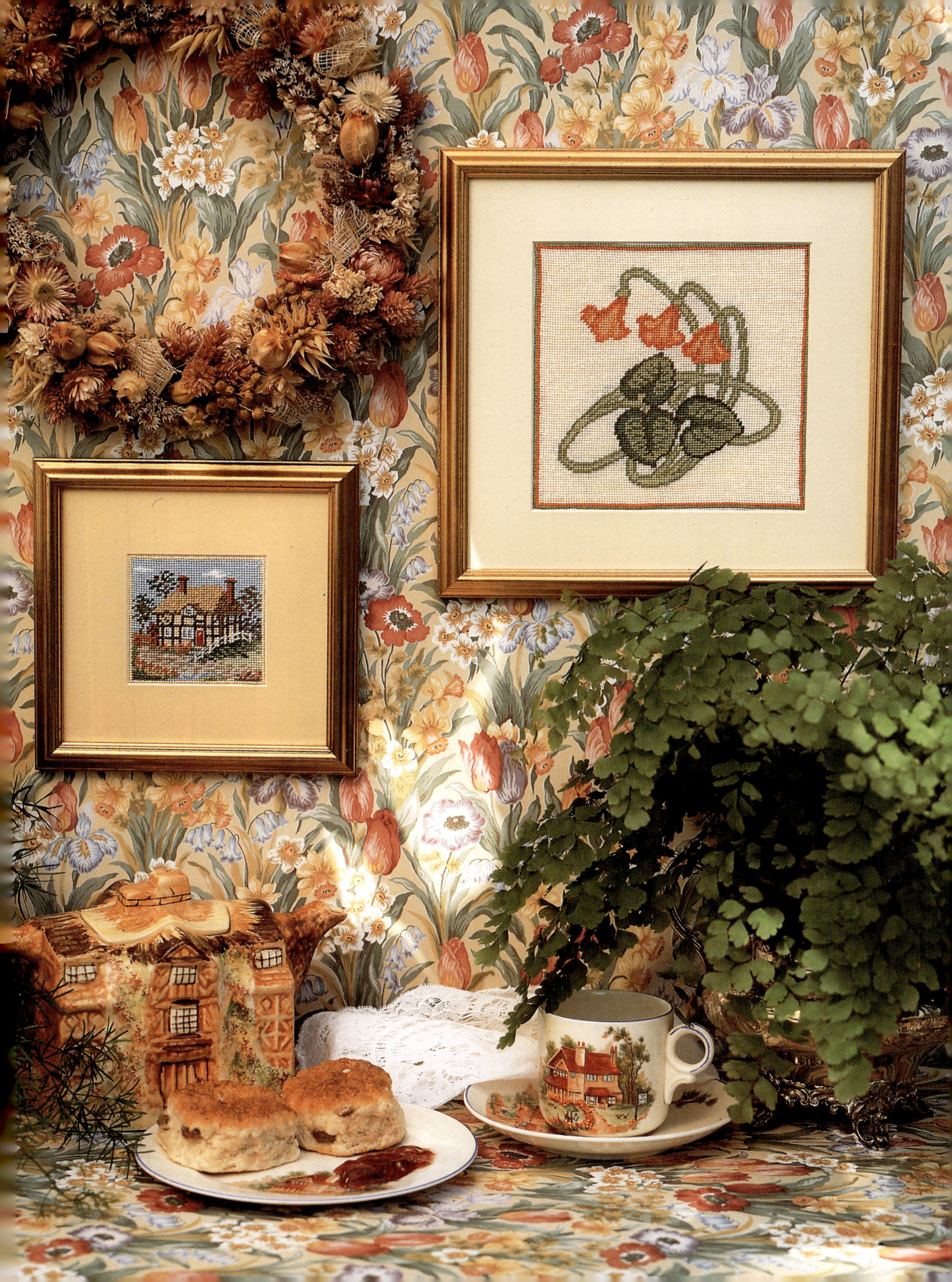

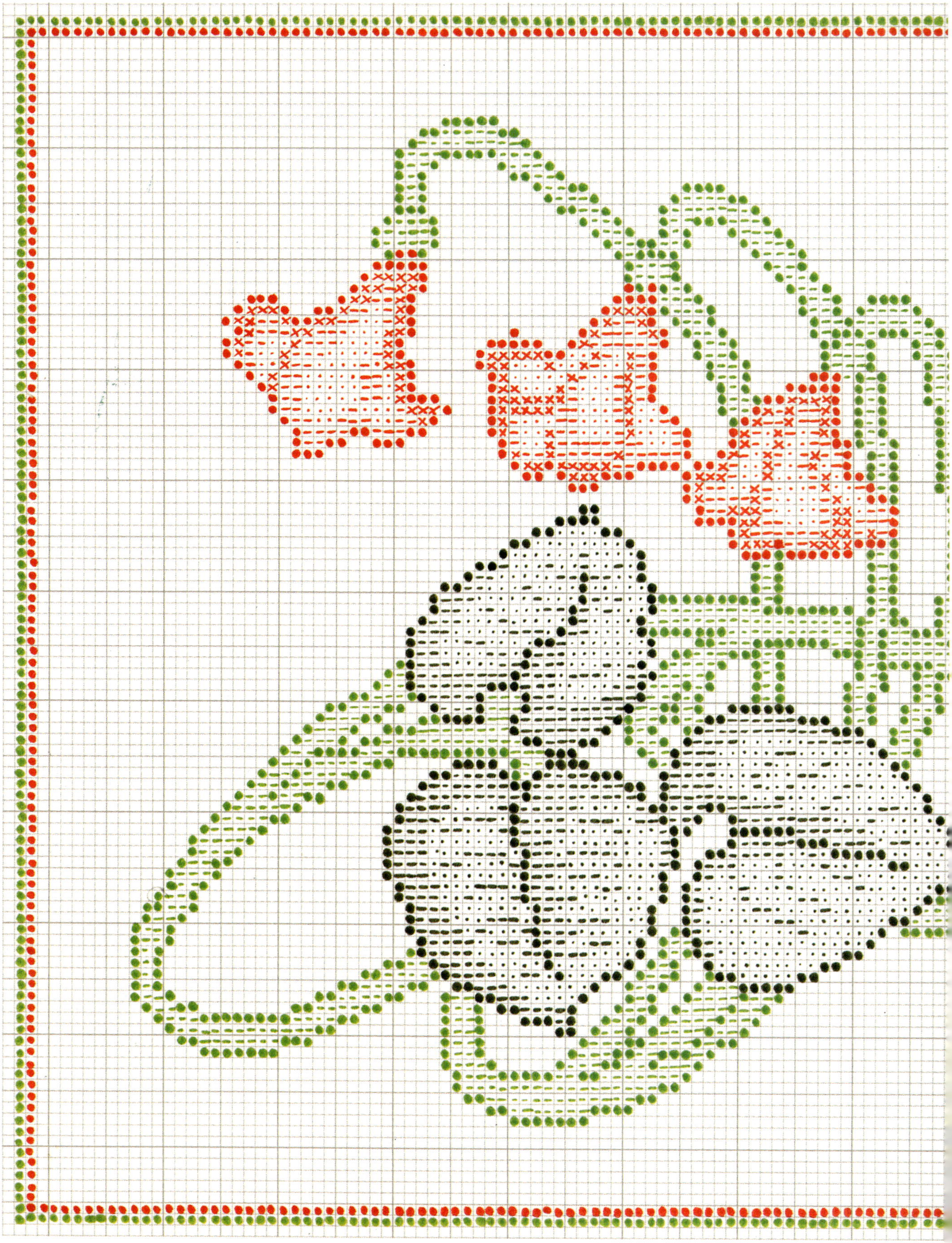

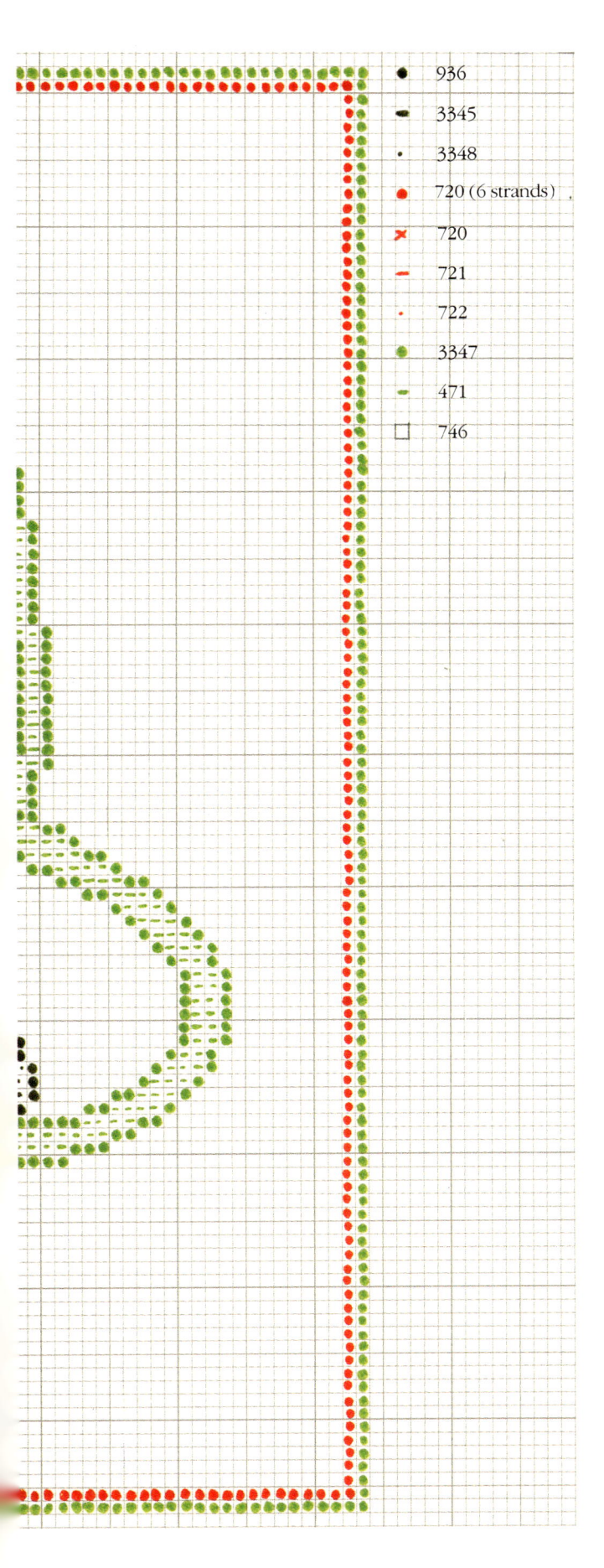

Chart key:
- ● 936
- ▬ 3345
- · 3348
- ● 720 (6 strands)
- ✗ 720
- — 721
- · 722
- ● 3347
- — 471
- ☐ 746

CANTERBURY BELLS

Elegant flowing foliage surrounds these delicate bell flowers to create a simple yet strong design.

NEEDLE Size 22
CANVAS 18 holes per inch (7 holes per cm)
SIZE OF CANVAS 10 x 10in (250 x 250mm)
SIZE OF FINISHED DESIGN 6 x 6in (150 x 150mm)
☐ Stranded cotton (floss) and cotton perlé (pearl cotton) as listed on the chart key

1 Find the centre point on the canvas and position the design as described in Basic Techniques.
2 Count from the centre point to the base of the middle flower and start stitching here. Six strands are used for the border of the flowers to give more depth to the design. Sew the three flowers, filling in the shading.
3 Starting at the top of the outside flower, stitch the stems working first the cotton perlé borders and then the leaves. Then fill in the details.
4 Stitch the border with one row of orange 720 in 6 strands and one row of green cotton perlé.
5 Work the background in cream 746.
6 The project shown was mounted and framed professionally with a pale cream mount and an antiqued 'old gold' wooden frame.

DMC	COLOUR	ANCHOR
3345	Dark Green	268
3348	Light Green	265
471	Green	255
720	Dark Orange	326
721	Orange	925
722	Pale Orange	314
746	Cream background (4 skeins)	386
936	Dark Green Perlé No. 5	846
3347	Green Perlé No. 5	266

PANSY

The deep purples in this charming pansy miniature, adapted from a Victorian card 'scrap', are typical of the period.

NEEDLE Size 22
CANVAS 18 holes per inch (7 holes per cm)
SIZE OF CANVAS 6 x 7in (150 x 180mm)
SIZE OF FINISHED DESIGN 2¾ x 3in (70 x 75mm)
☐ Stranded cottons (floss) and cotton perlé (pearl cotton) as listed on chart key

1 Find the centre point on the canvas and position the design as described in Basic Techniques.
2 Count the number of stitches from the centre point to the centre of the large pansy and start stitching here. Work colour by colour and then fill in the background and the outside border.
3 Work 1 strand of dark purple in backstitch to outline petals.
4 This project was professionally mounted and framed using an olive green mount and an 'old gold' moulded wood frame.

DMC	COLOUR	ANCHOR
550	Dark Purple	102
208	Purple	111
209	Light Purple	110
210	Very Pale Purple	109
3345	Dark Green	268
3346	Green	267
3347	Light Green	266
601	Pink	78
742	Gold	303
772	Pale Green background	253
936	Green Perlé No. 5	846

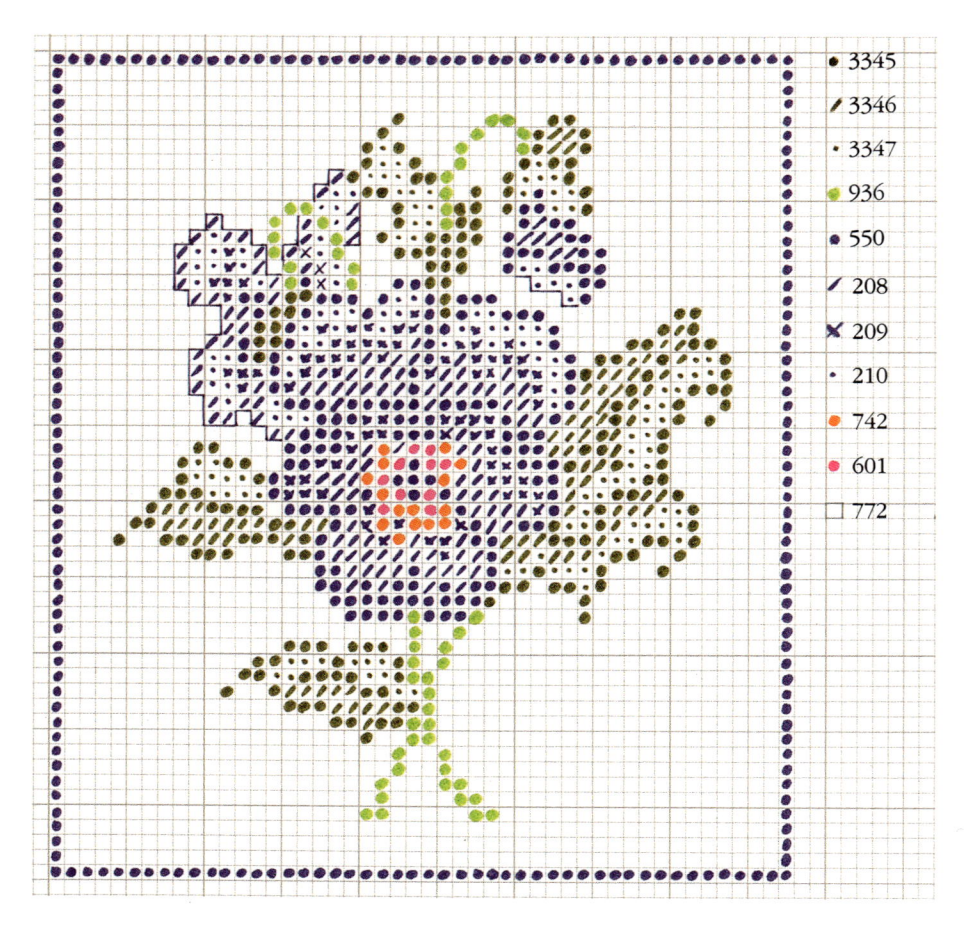

RED CAMPION

This miniature picture makes a pretty companion to the pansy.

NEEDLE Size 22
CANVAS 18 holes per inch (7 holes per cm)
SIZE OF CANVAS 6 x 7in (150 x 180mm)
SIZE OF FINISHED DESIGN 2¾ x 3in (70 x 75mm)
☐ Stranded cottons (floss) as listed on chart key

1 Find the centre point on the canvas and position the design as described in Basic Techniques.
2 Count the number of stitches from the centre point to the centre of the large pink flowers, start stitching here. Work colour by colour, then fill in the background colour and the outside border.
3 Work 1 strand of burgundy 321 in backstitch to outline petals where shown on the chart.
4 Use 2 strands of brown 300 to make the butterfly's antennae.
5 This project was professionally mounted and framed using an olive green mount and an 'old gold' moulded wood frame.

DMC	COLOUR	ANCHOR
321	Burgundy	047
3346	Green	267
3347	Light Green	266
3345	Dark Green	268
335	Dark Pink	41
899	Pink	52
3326	Pale Pink	25
743	Pale Gold	305
745	Cream	300
300	Brown	352
970	Orange	316
772	Pale Green background	253

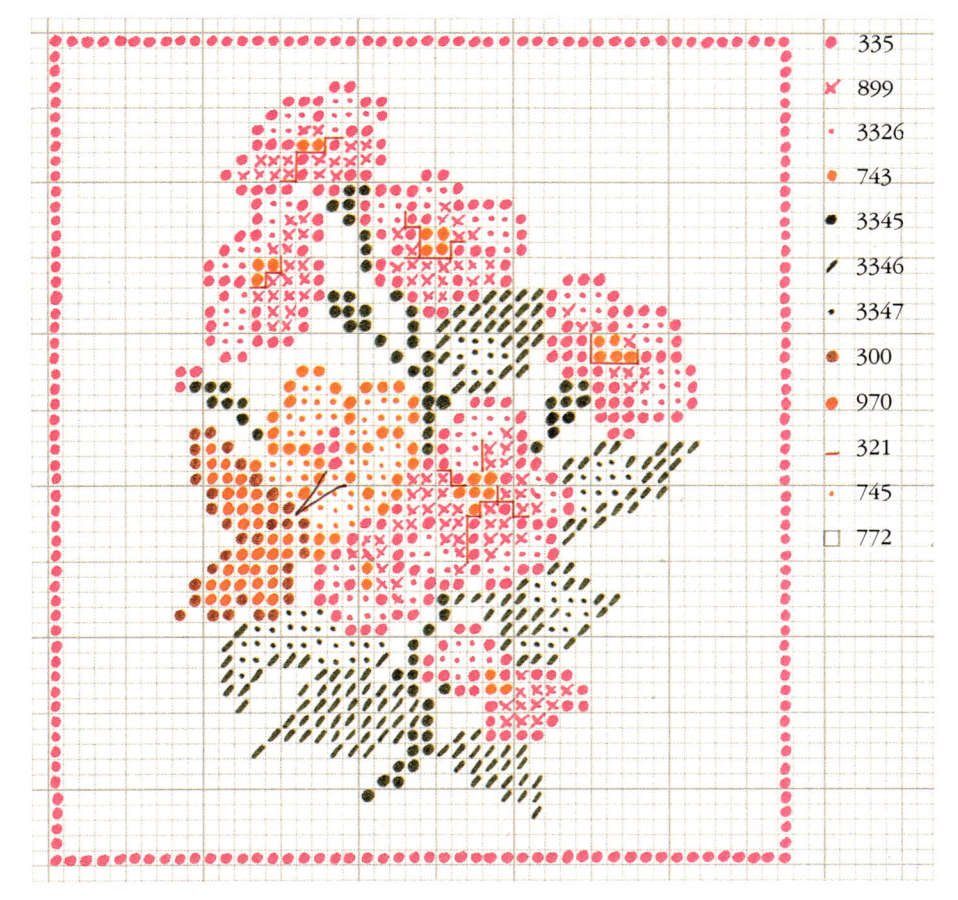

(Overleaf) Pansy, Red Campion and Poppy Tiles

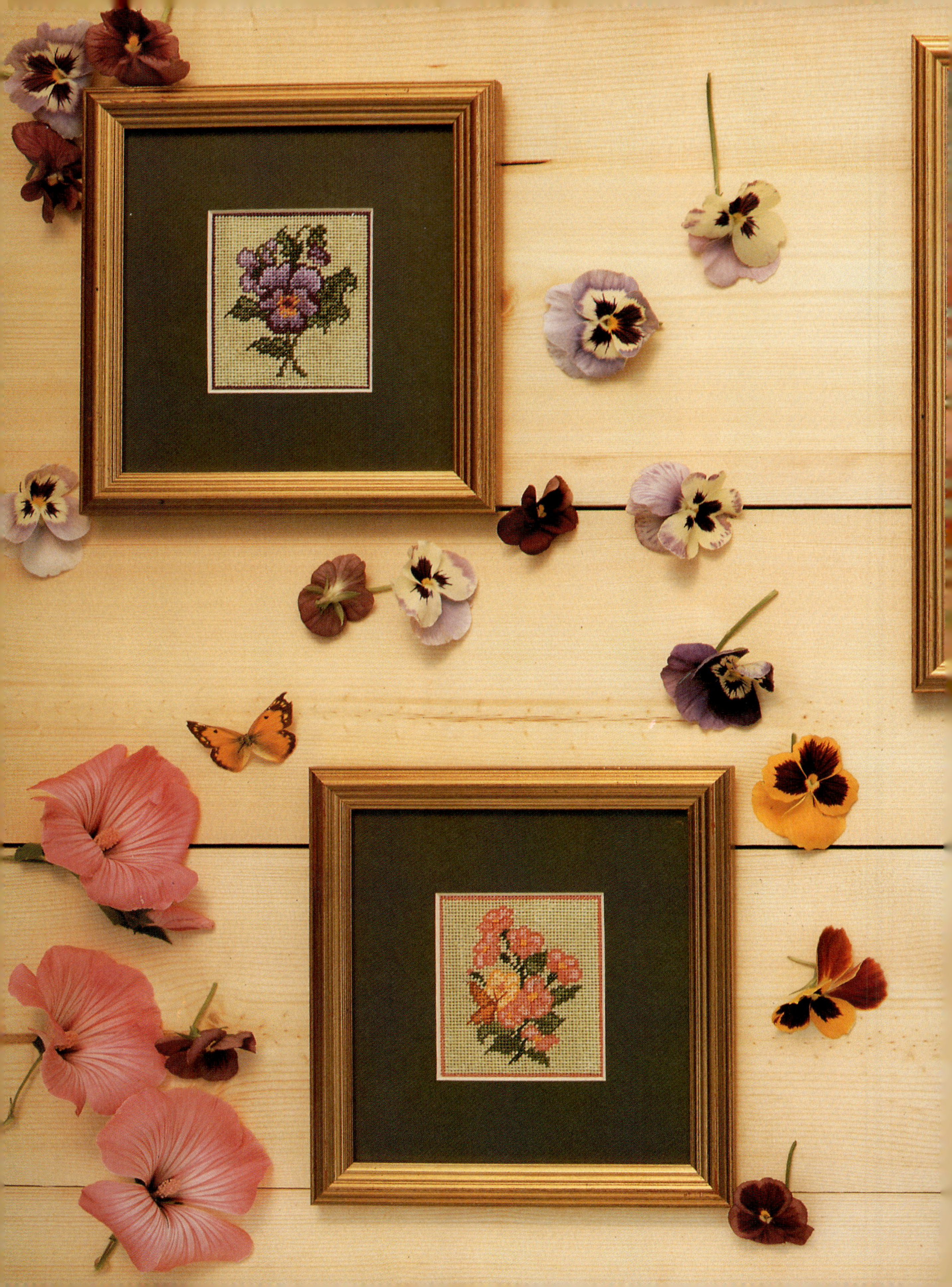

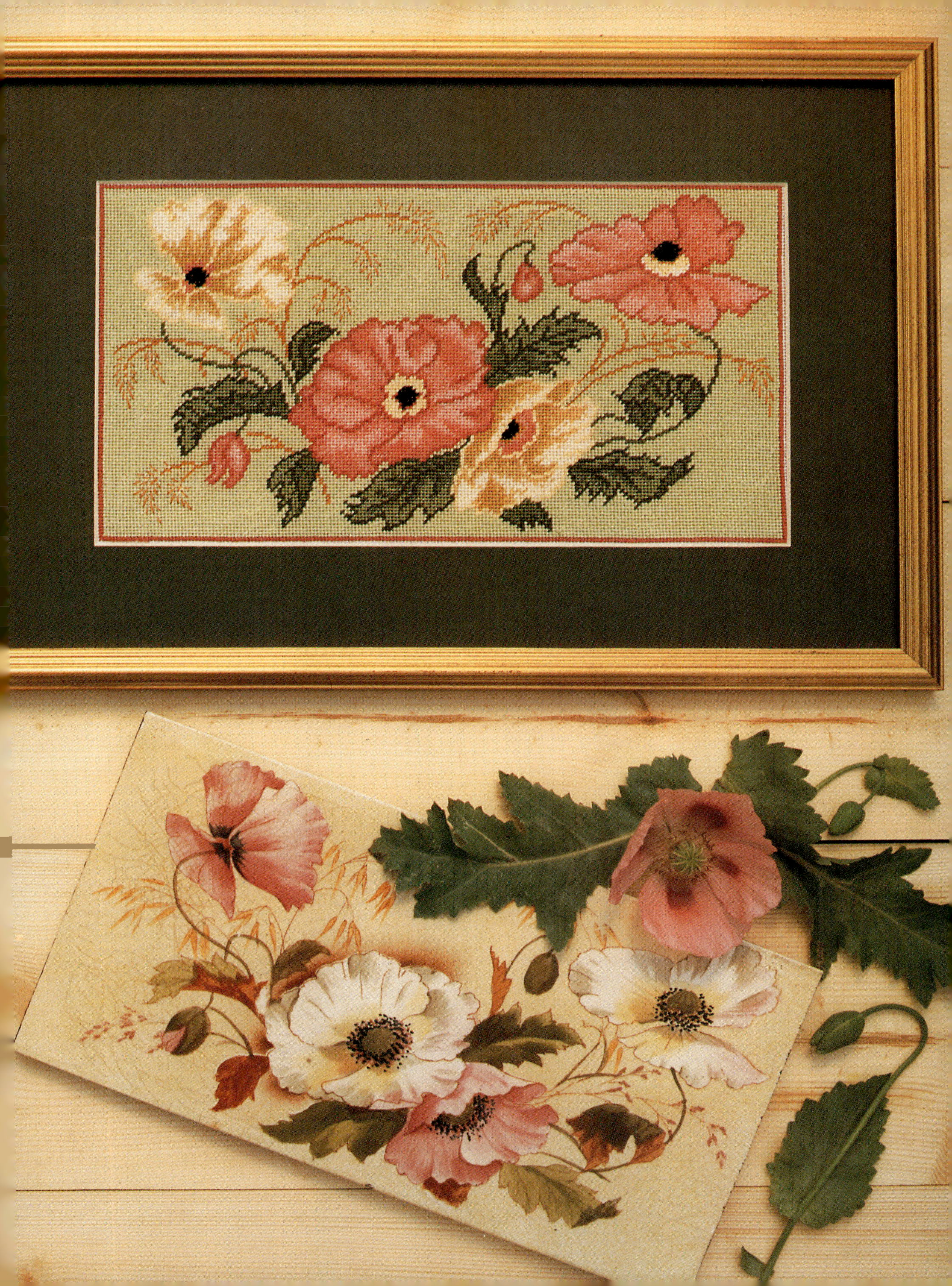

• 3350　• 335　• 899　• 3326　• 319　× 936　╱ 3346　• 3347　• 745　• 310　• 782　• 729　╱ 676　□ Blanc

Pink Poppy Tile

75

PINK POPPY TILE

Bending ears of wheat mingle with the bold flowers and foliage of poppies in this adaptation of a Victorian tile design.

NEEDLE Size 22
CANVAS 18 holes to the inch (7 holes per cm)
SIZE OF CANVAS 10 x 16in (250 x 400mm)
SIZE OF FINISHED DESIGN 6 x 11⅛in (150 x 283mm)
☐ Stranded cotton (floss) and cotton perlé (pearl cotton) as listed on the chart key

1   Find the centre point on the canvas and position the design as described in Basic Techniques.
2   Using the chart on pages 74–75, count the number of stitches from the centre point to the black centre of the large pink poppy. Start stitching here. Work the cotton perlé outlines for each flower before filling in the colours.
3   Stitch the background in very pale green 772 and then work the outer cotton perlé border.
4   Oversew the ears of wheat using 2 strands of dark ochre 782.
5   Mount and frame as preferred. This project was professionally framed in a moulded gilt frame with an olive green mount.

DMC	COLOUR	ANCHOR
782	Dark Ochre	307
729	Ochre	890
676	Pale Ochre	891
Blanc	White	01
335	Dark Pink	41
899	Pink	52
3326	Pale Pink	25
319	Dark Green	212
3346	Green	267
3347	Pale Green	266
310	Black	403
772	Very Pale Green background (5 skeins)	253
3350	Pink Perlé No. 5	42
936	Green Perlé No. 5	846
745	Cream Perlé No. 5	300

THATCHED COTTAGE

This idyllic cottage nestles under a blue sky in a typically English country garden in full bloom.

NEEDLE Size 22
CANVAS 18 holes per inch (7 holes per cm)
SIZE OF CANVAS 6 x 6in (150 x 150mm)
SIZE OF FINISHED DESIGN 3 x 3in (76 x 76mm)
☐ Stranded cottons (floss) and cotton perlé (pearl cotton) as listed on the chart key

1   Find the centre point on the canvas and position the design as described in Basic Techniques.
2   Count from the centre point to the main horizontal beam of the house and start stitching here. Work colour by colour. Complete the house before working the garden and background details.
3   Stitch the border in cotton perlé.
4   To complete the design oversew window details with 1 strand of dark blue 336, the door border with 1 strand of white, the corner of the house with 1 strand of dark ochre 829 and the attic window frame with one strand of dark brown 3031. Use 1 strand of black 310 for the large window frame base. The fence posts are linked by oversewing two parallel rows using two strands of white thread.
5   The picture shown on page 67 was mounted and framed professionally using a deep cream mount and an 'old gold' mounted wood frame.

DMC	COLOUR	ANCHOR	DMC	COLOUR	ANCHOR
415	Light Grey	398	743	Yellow	305
317	Dark Grey	400	745	Cream	300
3033	Beige	390	899	Light Pink	52
3032	Dark Beige	392	335	Pink	41
301	Brown	349	309	Dark Pink	39
3031	Dark Brown	380	210	Pale Purple	109
676	Light Ochre	891	208	Purple	111
680	Dark Ochre	901	794	Blue	129
829	Very Dark Ochre	906	800	Pale Blue	128
300	Chocolate Brown	352	336	Dark Blue	148
3345	Dark Green	268	775	Very Pale Blue	158
3346	Mid Green	267	666	Red	46
3347	Green	266	Blanc	White	01
3348	Light Green	265	310	Black	403
772	Very Light Green	253	745	Cream Perlé No. 5	300
471	Lime Green	254			

VICTORIAN POSY BOX

Transform a plain wooden box into a decorative accessory with this design of a basket of roses.

NEEDLE Size 22
CANVAS 18 holes per inch (7 holes per cm)
SIZE OF CANVAS 8 x 8in (200 x 200mm)
SIZE OF FINISHED DESIGN 4 x 4in (100 x 100mm)
- Stranded cottons (floss) as listed on the chart key
- Wadding (Batting)
- 4½in (115mm) square wooden box with approx. ¼in (5mm) recess in lid
- Craft glue (PVA)
- Thin cardboard

1 Find the centre point on the canvas and position the design as described in Basic Techniques.
2 Count from the centre point to the top edge of the basket. Stitch the basket.
3 Stitch the flowers and foliage.
4 Using 1 strand of dark pink 309 outline the right-hand rose in backstitch.
5 Complete by stitching the cream background. The background can be increased or reduced for different-sized boxes.
6 To place the picture in the lid cut a piece of wadding slightly smaller than the overall size of the stitched canvas.

7 Trim the canvas to ¾in (20mm) all around. Cut diagonally across the corners, not too close to the stitches. Fold the unworked canvas over the wadding at the stitched line and press down firmly to create a stiff folded edge. Cut a piece of thin cardboard to size. Glue the card to the canvas and wadding. Use more glue to anchor the needlepoint inside the recess of the box lid.

Victorian Posy Lid, Butterfly Needlecase and Pincushion

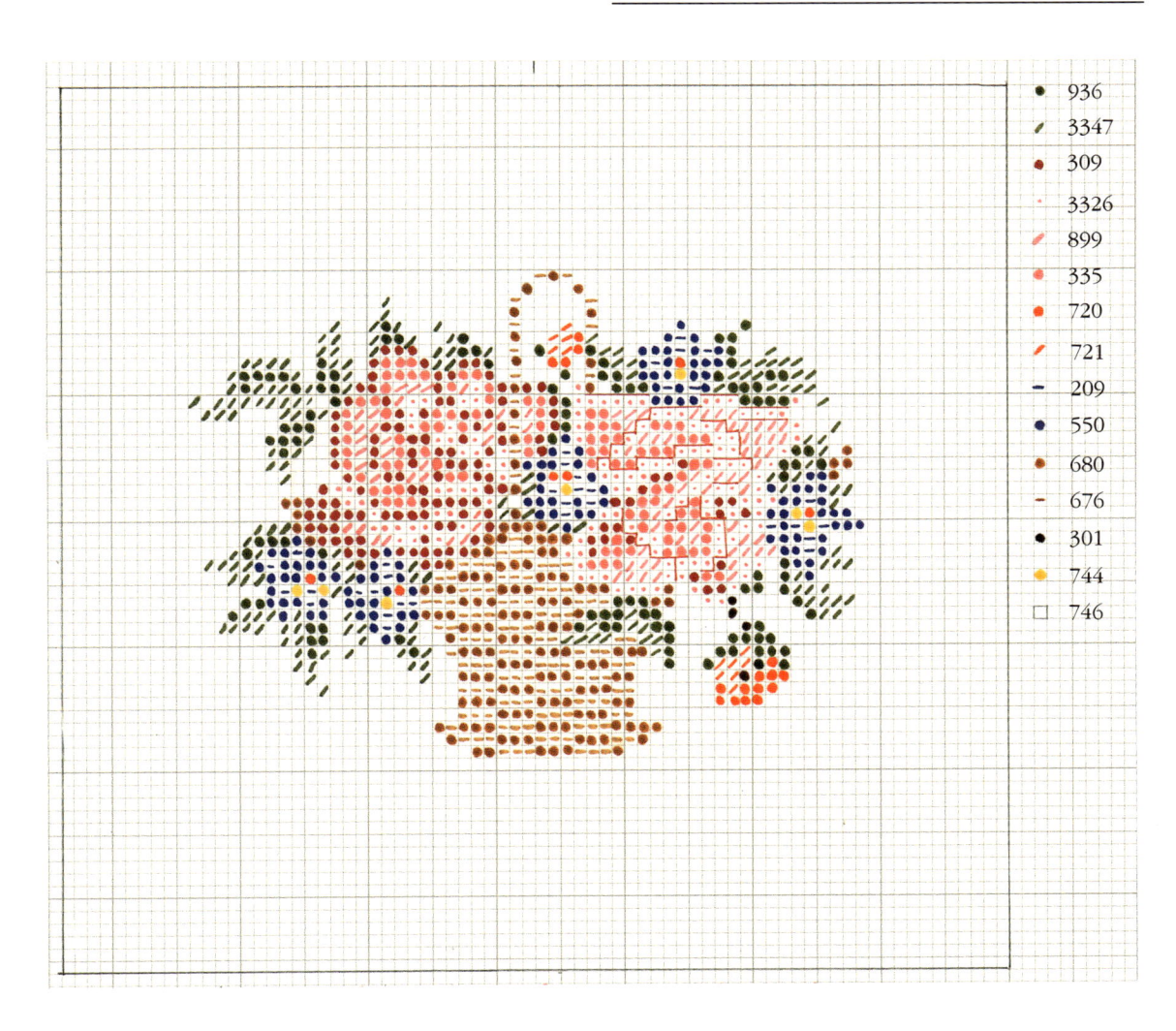

DMC	COLOUR	ANCHOR
744	Yellow	295
680	Dark Ochre	901
676	Light Ochre	891
936	Dark Green	846
3347	Green	266
550	Purple	102
209	Light Purple	110
720	Orange	326
721	Light Orange	925
3326	Very Pale Pink	25
899	Pale Pink	52
335	Pink	41
309	Dark Pink	39
301	Brown	349
746	Cream background (2 skeins)	386

- ● 936
- ╱ 3347
- ● 309
- · 3326
- ╱ 899
- ● 335
- ● 720
- ╱ 721
- − 209
- ● 550
- ● 680
- − 676
- ● 301
- ● 744
- □ 746

BUTTERFLY NEEDLECASE

The butterfly shape with its opening and closing wings lends itself particularly well to this needlecase and makes a companion piece to the pincushion. (See chart overleaf)

NEEDLE Size 22
CANVAS 18 holes per inch (7 holes per cm)
SIZE OF CANVAS 9 x 6½in (230 x 165mm)
SIZE OF FINISHED DESIGN 6 x 4in (150 x 100mm)
☐ Stranded cottons (floss) as listed on the chart key
☐ Black backing fabric 9 x 6in (230 x 150mm)
☐ Black felt 7 x 6in (180 x 150mm)
☐ Tracing paper
☐ Black ribbon ⅛in (3mm) wide x 12in (300mm) long

1 Find the centre point on the canvas and position the design as described in Basic Techniques.
2 Count the number of stitches from the centre point to the nearest butterfly and start stitching here. Work colour by colour, stitching the background last, using 5 strands of black 310.
3 Block the needlepoint as described in Basic Techniques.
4 Trim the canvas to ¼in (5mm) all around the edge.
5 With the right sides of the needlepoint and piece of backing fabric facing, pin in place. Backstitch all around the edge of the butterfly as close to the stitching as possible. Leave an opening as indicated on the diagram.

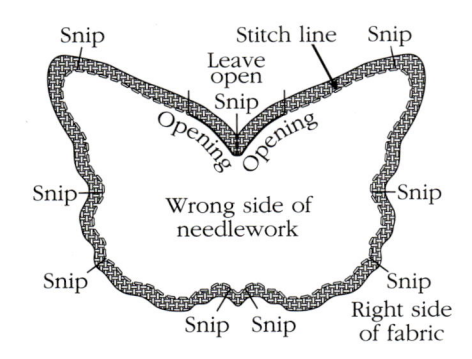

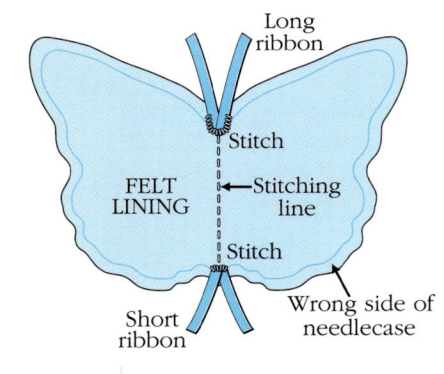

FELT TEMPLATE
Fold

DMC	COLOUR	ANCHOR
996	Pale Turquoise	433
995	Turquoise	410
970	Orange	316
208	Purple	110
601	Pink	78
907	Green	255
742	Gold	303
676	Ochre	891
310	Black background (4 skeins)	403

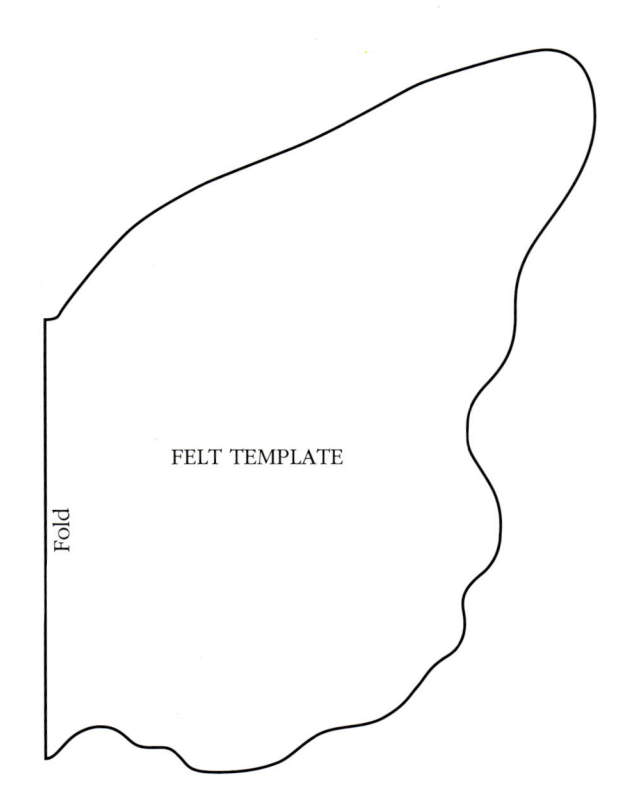

6 Carefully snip the edges as shown and trim the backing fabric to ¼in (5mm) all around.
7 Turn inside out and press gently with a steam iron, easing out the corners. Fold in the canvas and fabric at the opening and sew up neatly.
8 Trace the template for the felt and cut out one black felt butterfly.
9 Cut two lengths of the black ribbon, one 7in (180mm) long and the other 4in (100mm) long. Fold the longest piece in half and stitch to the needlecase as shown to form the antennae. Fold the short piece in half and stitch as shown. Stitch felt on needlecase.

BUTTERFLY PINCUSHION

The bright colours and black background make this design very striking. If you use unwashed sheep's wool to stuff the pincushion, the oil in the fleece protects the pins from rusting. (See chart overleaf)

NEEDLE Size 22
CANVAS 18 holes to the inch (7 holes per cm)
SIZE OF CANVAS 7½in (190mm) square
SIZE OF FINISHED DESIGN 4¾in (120mm) square
☐ Stranded cottons (floss) as listed on the chart key
☐ Black backing fabric 7½in (190mm) square
☐ Stuffing – unwashed sheep's wool or kapok

1 Find centre point on the canvas and position the design as described in Basic Techniques.
2 Count the number of stitches from the centre point to one butterfly and start stitching here. Work colour by colour, stitching the background last, using 5 strands of black 310. Use 1 strand of black to backstitch the division between each pair of wings.
3 Block your needlework as described in Basic Techniques.
4 With right sides of the backing fabric and needlepoint facing, pin in place.
5 Backstitch around the edge of the pincushion as close to the needlepoint stitches as possible, leaving an opening 2½in (60mm) long as shown. Trim the edges to ¼in (5mm) and cut across the corners.
6 Turn inside out and ease out the corners. Press gently from the back with a steam iron. Fill with stuffing and sew up the opening.

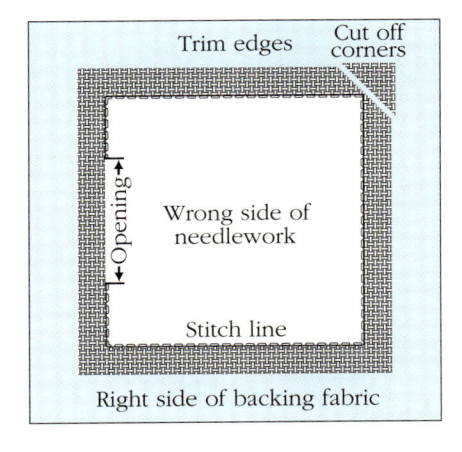

DMC	COLOUR	ANCHOR
996	Turquoise	433
970	Orange	316
208	Purple	111
601	Pink	78
907	Green	255
742	Gold	303
676	Ochre	891
310	Black background (4 skeins)	403

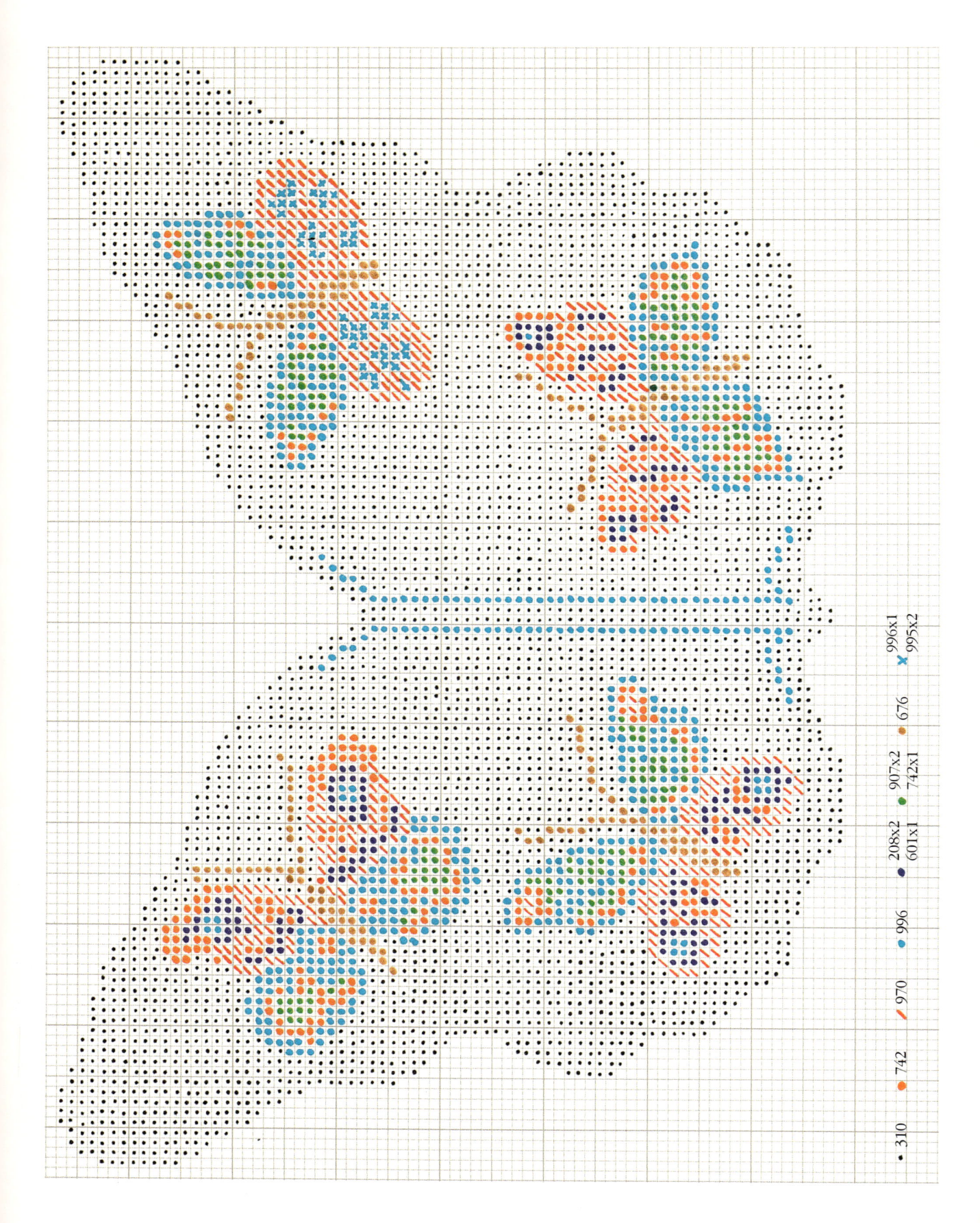

- 310
- 742
| 970
• 996
• 208x2
• 601x1
• 907x2
/ 742x1
• 676
• 996x1
✗ 995x2

• 996 ✗ 742 • 208x2 601x1 • 970 ✗ 676 • 907x2 742x1 • 310

(Opposite) Butterfly Needlecase;
(Above) Butterfly Pincushion

Chapter 6

Decorative Ideas

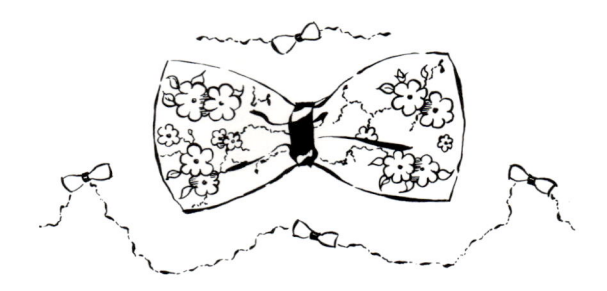

Although needlepoint designs make lovely pictures to be admired for generations to come, there are other novel ways in which needlepoint may be used. Most civilizations throughout history have had some form of traditional handsewn needlework. In Britain the Elizabethan age saw a surge of interest in decorative stitched items. The projects in this chapter are small, delicate pieces for you and your home.

We all have a favourite photo and a pretty frame in needlepoint will make it extra special. The miniature rose frame in delicate shades of pink would also make a lovely gift, or with a mirror placed in the centre would be an attractive accessory. The colours can be adapted to suit the decor of any room.

The idea for the little thatched cottage came from a rather old and faded needlepoint tea cosy unearthed in a local antique market. We reduced the size, brightened the colours and gave the flowers more detail. Filled with lavender, it became a novel pot pourri holder.

Picture bows, which provide a decorative way to hang small pictures and photographs, have become popular with the revival of Victorian decorative ideas. Old fabrics and wallpapers can provide an endless source of inspiration for floral motifs and hunting for ideas can become an integral part of the enjoyment of needlework. Our Picture Bow, based on a lovely piece of curtain fabric which once belonged to Judy's grandmother, can, like most designs, be worked in your choice of colourways.

The hair bow is a geometric design using three strong colours and gold metallic thread to give it a festive party look. The squares can be worked in any colour you like to coordinate with a particular outfit.

Floral Border Picture Frame

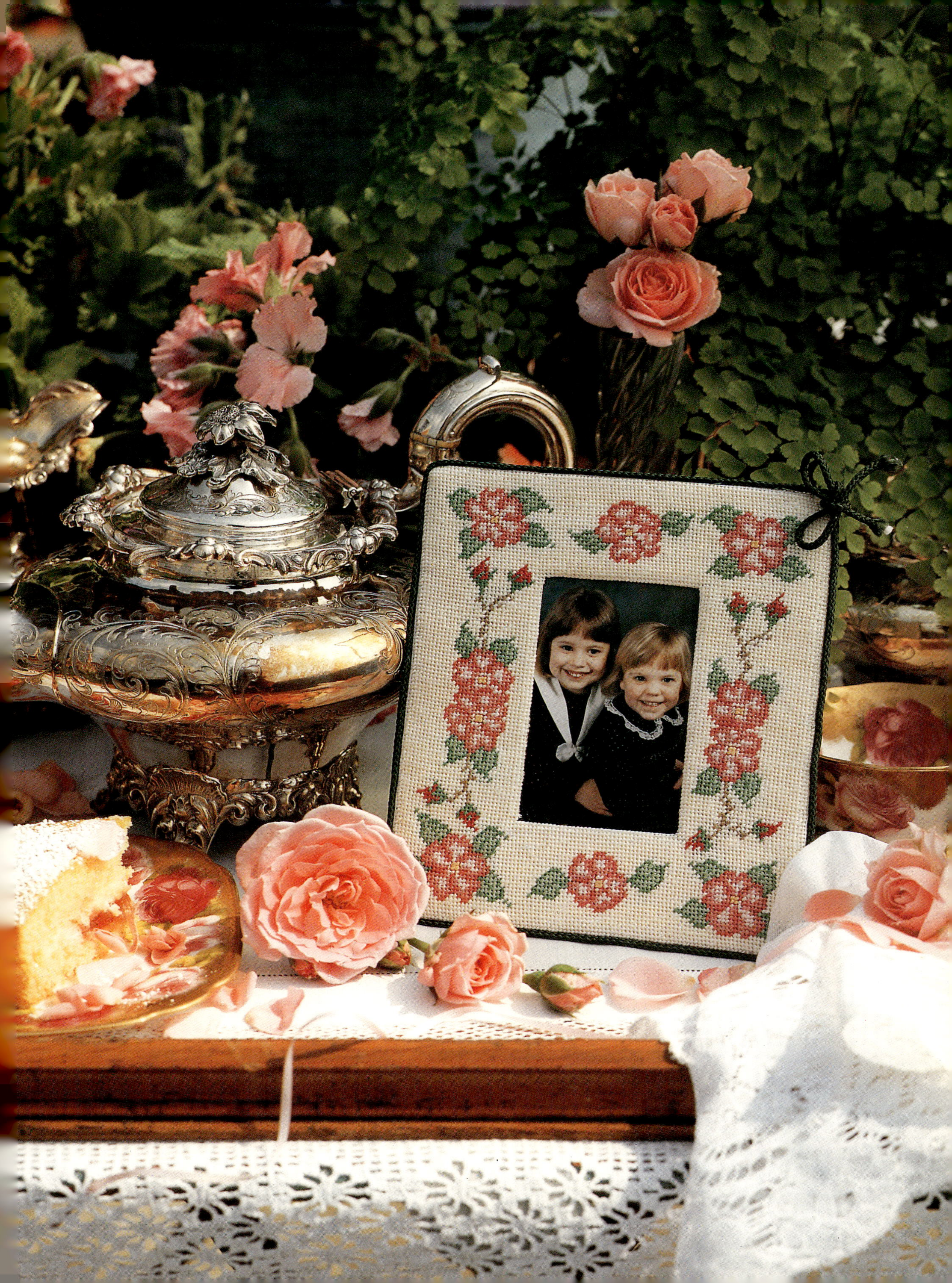

Floral Frame

This Wild Rose Border would make a very pretty picture frame for a special photo or a mirror mount for a dressing table.

NEEDLE Size 22
CANVAS 18 holes to the inch (7 holes per cm)
SIZE OF CANVAS 9 x 9½in (230 x 240mm)
SIZE OF FINISHED DESIGN 5¾ x 6½in (146 x 165mm)

- Stranded cottons (floss) as listed on chart key
- Mount card (mat board) 5¾ x 6½in (146 x 165mm)
- 30in (750mm) length of braid
- Cotton fabric 8 x 9in (200 x 230mm)
- Thin cardboard 5½ x 6in (140 x 150mm)
- Craft knife
- Craft glue (PVA)

1 Find the centre point on the canvas and position the design as described in Basic Techniques.
2 From the centre point count to the bottom of the centre top flower. Start stitching here.
3 Work colour by colour completing the flowers and leaves. Do not work the centre rectangle marked on the chart.
4 Stitch the cream background. Highlight the flowers as shown on the chart using backstitch and one strand of dark pink (309).
5 To make up: Seal the inside edge of the canvas as near as possible to the stitching with Fray Check. With a sharp pair of scissors pierce the centre of the canvas and cut diagonal lines into the four inside corners. Trim the canvas to ½in (12mm) around the inside and outside edges of the worked area. Snip across the four outside corners as shown.
6 Cut the centre opening 2¼ x 3½in (55 x 90mm) in the mount card. Ideally this inside edge should be bevelled and the outside edge reverse-bevelled. A professional framer could cut these edges if you prefer.
7 Place the needlepoint onto the mount card and fold edges of the canvas gently over the card. Use strong craft glue to stick the raw edges of the canvas to the back of the mount card as tightly as possible and leave to dry.
8 Starting at the top right-hand corner, leaving a tail of 6in (150mm), attach the braid to the edge of the canvas with running stitch. Tie a bow with the tail ends and trim.
9 Cut the backing fabric ¼in (5mm) larger than the finished canvas size. Press under ¼in (5mm) all around. Stitch in place on the back of the mount with whipstitch, leaving the top open. For added strength insert a piece of thin cardboard into the opening of the pocket at the top.

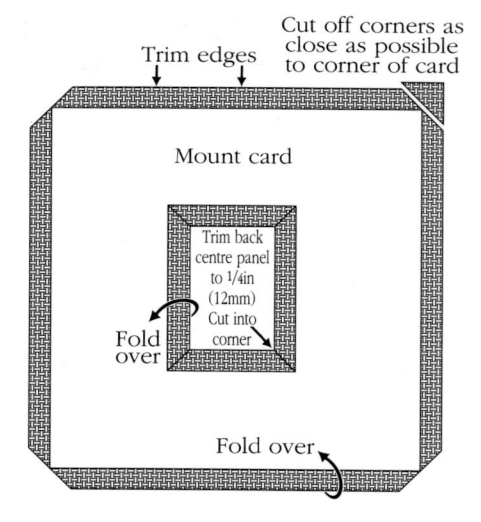

DMC	COLOUR	ANCHOR
954	Light Green	203
912	Green	205
335	Pink	41
899	Pale Pink	52
818	Very Pale Pink	48
309	Dark Pink	39
744	Yellow	295
3022	Brown	392
746	Cream background (3 skeins)	386

• 335   • 899   • 818   • 309   • 744   • 912   • 954   • 3022   □ 746

PICTURE BOW

The bow in our photograph is in pink on a cream background, while the chart shows an alternative bow in blue on white. Substitute three shades of any colour for the blues on the chart.

NEEDLE Size 22
CANVAS 18 holes to the inch (7 holes per cm)
SIZE OF CANVAS 10 x 7in (250 x 180mm)
SIZE OF FINISHED DESIGN 7½ x 4¼in (190 x 105mm)
- Stranded cottons (floss) as listed on chart key
- Satin ribbon ½in (12mm) wide x 1⅔yds (1.5m) long
- Cotton backing fabric 10 x 7in (250 x 180mm)
- Wadding (batting) 7½in x 4¼in (190 x 105mm)
- Small brass curtain ring

1 Find the centre point on the canvas and position the design as described in Basic Techniques.
2 Count the number of stitches from the centre point to the nearest flower and start stitching here. work colour by colour, stitching the background last. Note that there will be an unworked strip of canvas down the centre of the design.
3 Block the needlepoint as described in Basic Techniques.
4 Place the needlepoint and backing fabric right sides together. Using white cotton thread, back-stitch as close to the needlepoint as possible to attach the backing fabric to the canvas. Leave a 3in (75mm) gap at the bottom. Trim the edges to ¼in (5mm) and cut corners diagonally.

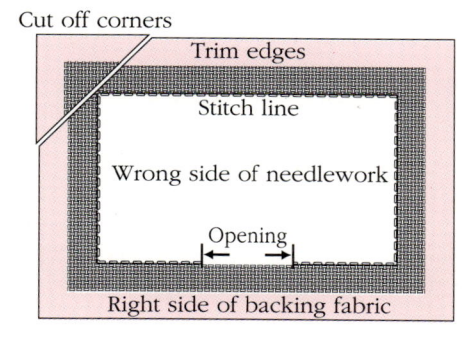

5 Turn inside out and press gently with a steam iron, easing out the corners. Push the wadding into the corners gently and sew up the opening.
6 Using 4 strands of thread, sew 2 rows of running stitches down the unworked centre strip. Secure the thread at one end with knots. Pull the threads to gather the bow evenly and secure firmly.

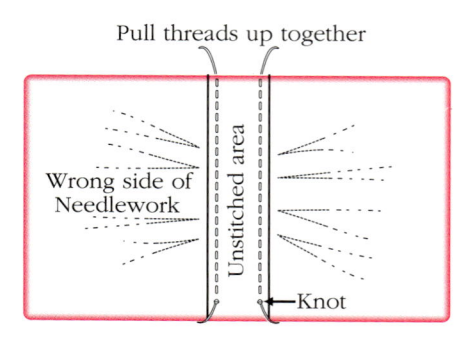

7 Wrap the ribbon around the centre of the bow and tie with a double knot, making sure the ribbons are of equal length, and trim the ends at a 45° angle to finish them neatly. Sew a small brass ring to the back of the bow for hanging.

DMC	COLOUR	ANCHOR
Blue Bow		
798	Dark Blue	131
800	Blue	128
775	Pale Blue	158
3347	Green	266
3346	Dark Green	267
772	Pale Green	253
3078	Lemon	292
Blanc	White background (3 skeins)	01
Pink Bow (substitute pinks for blues above)		
335	Dark Pink	41
899	Pink	52
3326	Pale Pink	25
746	Cream background (3 skeins)	386

Picture Bow and Home Sweet Home

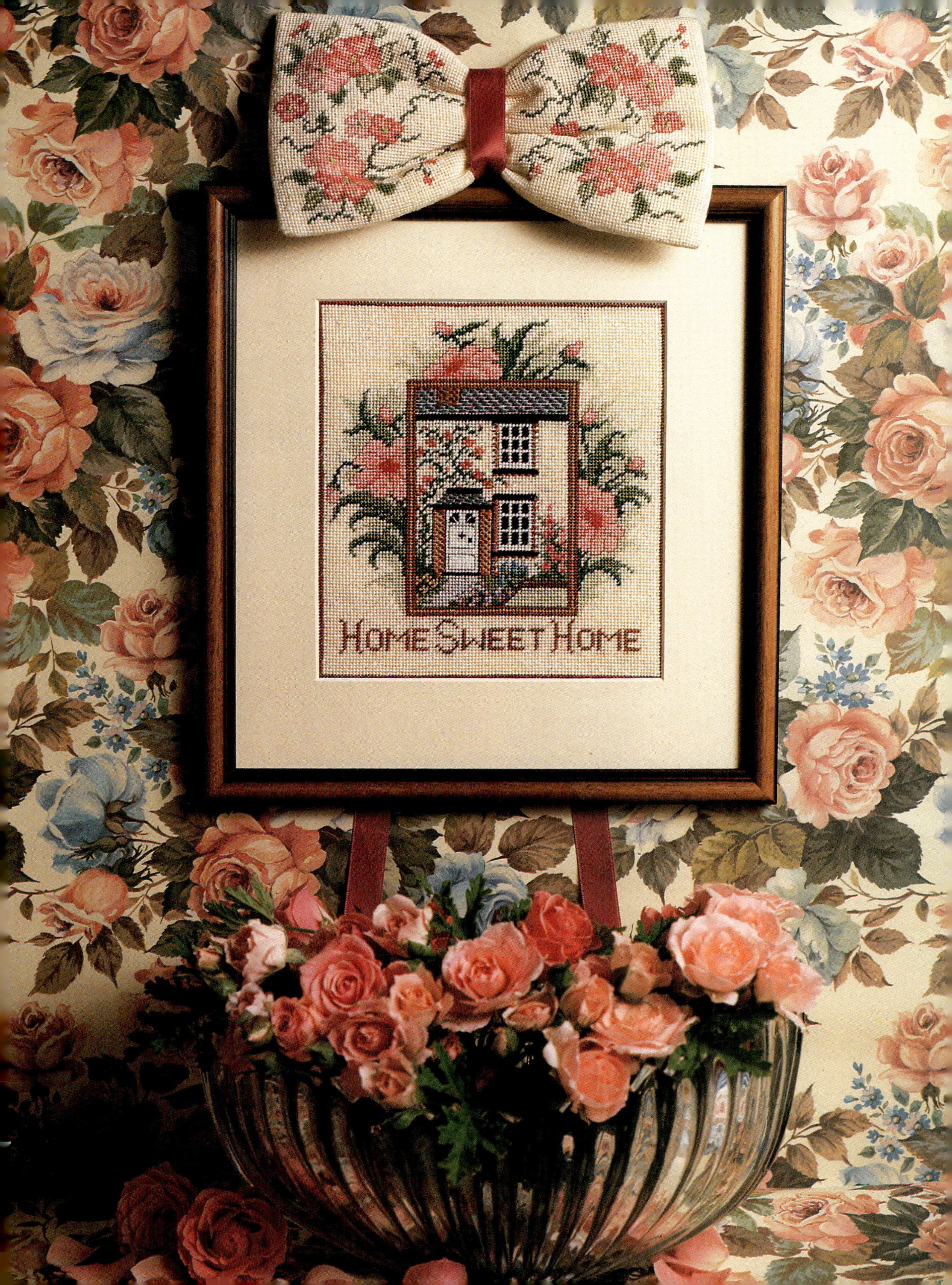
HOME SWEET HOME

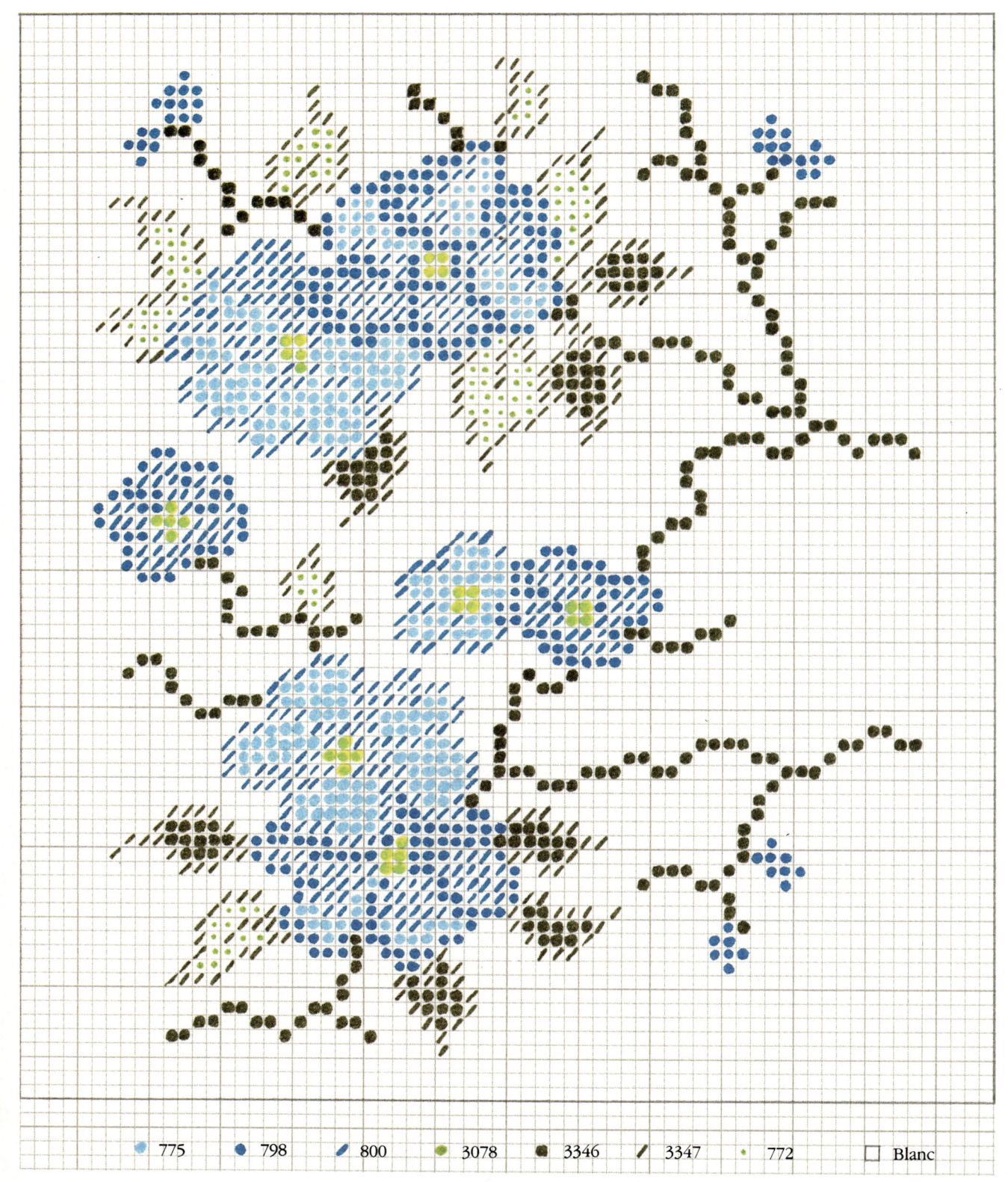

Picture Bow

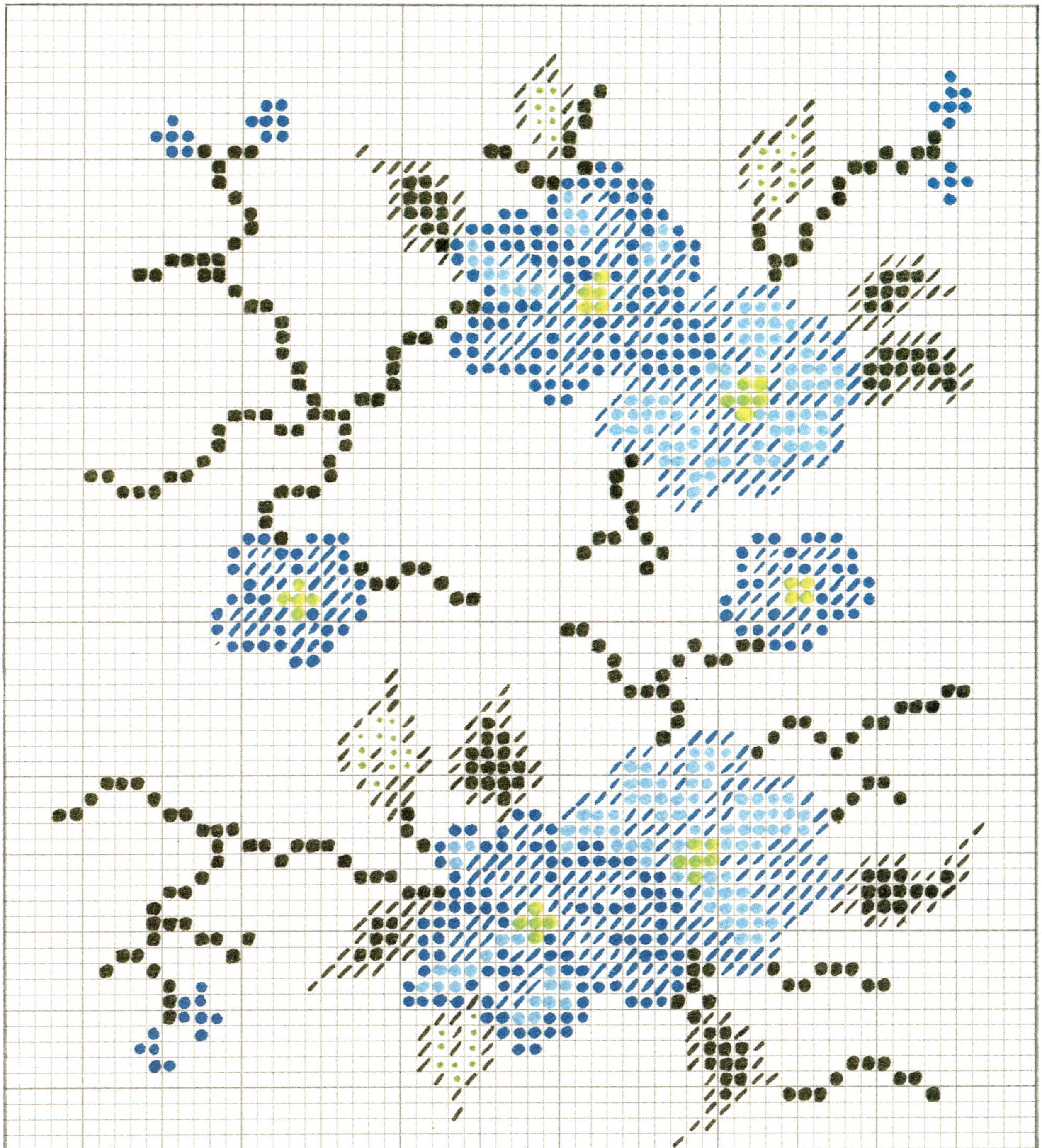

HAIR BOW

This striking geometric bow with gold thread highlights can be stitched like the photograph in red and blue, or like the chart in yellow and blue, or in any colours of your choice.

NEEDLE Size 22
CANVAS 18 holes to the inch (7 holes per cm)
SIZE OF CANVAS 6½ x 4¾in (165 x 120mm)
SIZE OF FINISHED DESIGN 5 x 3¼in (125 x 83mm)
▢ Stranded cottons (floss) as listed on the chart key
▢ Black lining fabric 6½ x 4¾in (165 x 120mm)
▢ Hair slide (Barette clip) 3in (75mm) long
▢ Ribbon to match ½in (12mm) wide x 6in (150mm) long
▢ Wadding (batting) 5 x 3¼in (125 x 83mm)

1   Find the centre point on the canvas and position the design as described in Basic Techniques.
2   Start by stitching the centre yellow diamond. Work colour by colour, stitching the metallic threads last.
3   Block your needlework as described in Basic Techniques.
4   Make up the bow as described on page 88, steps 4, 5 and 6.
5   Wrap the ribbon around the centre of the bow, and tie it neatly at the back. Trim the ends at an angle and stitch on to the hair slide.

DMC	COLOUR	ANCHOR
310	Black	403
Blanc	White	01
666	Red or	46
744	Yellow	295
995	Blue	410
MADEIRA	Madeira Gold	325

Hair Bow

● 325(Mad)	● 310
● 744	● 995
● 666	☐ Blanc

COUNTRY COTTAGE POT POURRI

This delightful 'chocolate box' thatched cottage with hollyhocks and wisteria is filled with sweetly scented pot pourri.

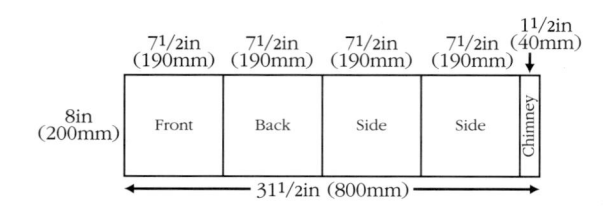

NEEDLE Size 22
CANVAS 18 holes to the inch (7 holes per cm)
SIZE OF CANVAS 8 x 31½in (200 x 800mm)
SIZE OF FINISHED DESIGN 4½in high x 4½in wide x 3in deep (115 x 115 x 75mm)
- Stranded cottons (floss) as listed on chart key
- Pot pourri
- 6in (150mm) square of muslin (cheesecloth)
- Wadding (batting)
- White felt 3¼ x 4¼in (83 x 108mm)

1 Cut the canvas into four sections as shown in the diagram, leaving a strip 1½in (40mm) wide. Choose the side of the cottage where you wish to begin and fold the canvas into four to find the centre point. Position the design as described in Basic Techniques.
2 Count the number of stitches from the centre point to a beam and start stitching here. Stitch colour by colour leaving the cream background until last. Work all 4 sides of the cottage in the same way.
3 Oversew the window panes using 1 strand of black 310 as shown on chart for cottage front. Use backstitch and 1 strand of black to outline the cat flap on the back door.
4 Block the needlepoint as described in Basic Techniques.

Pot Pourri Cottage

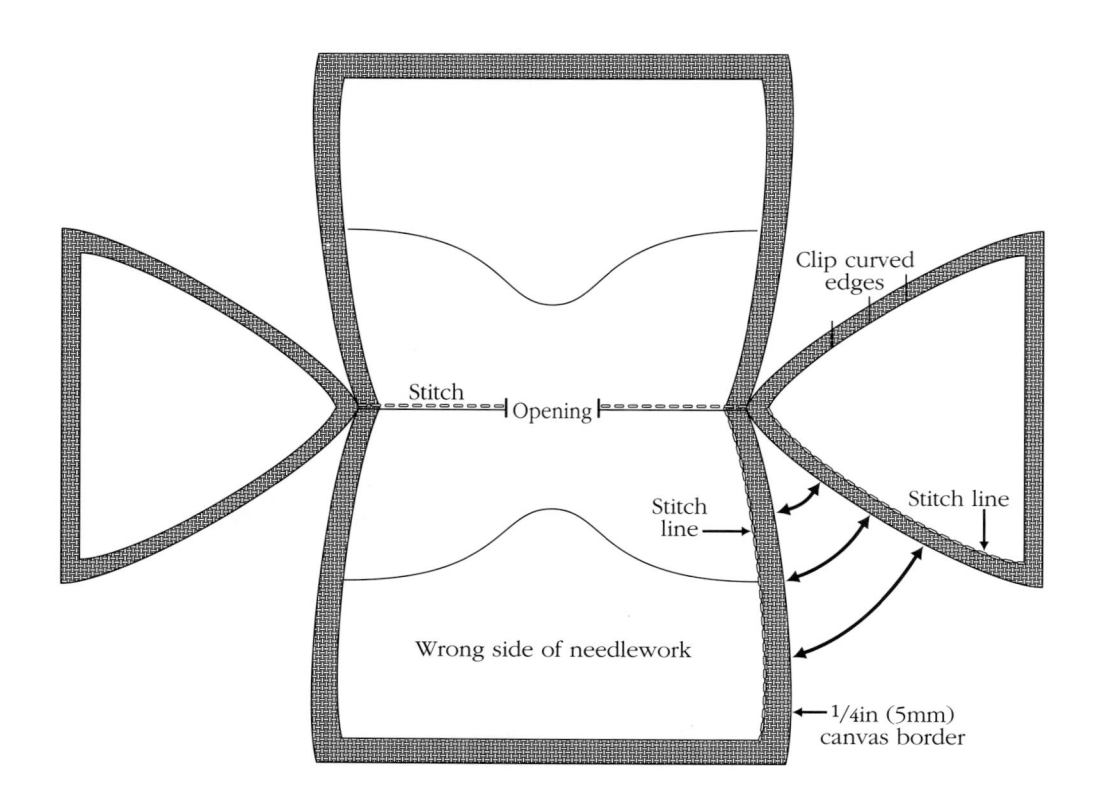

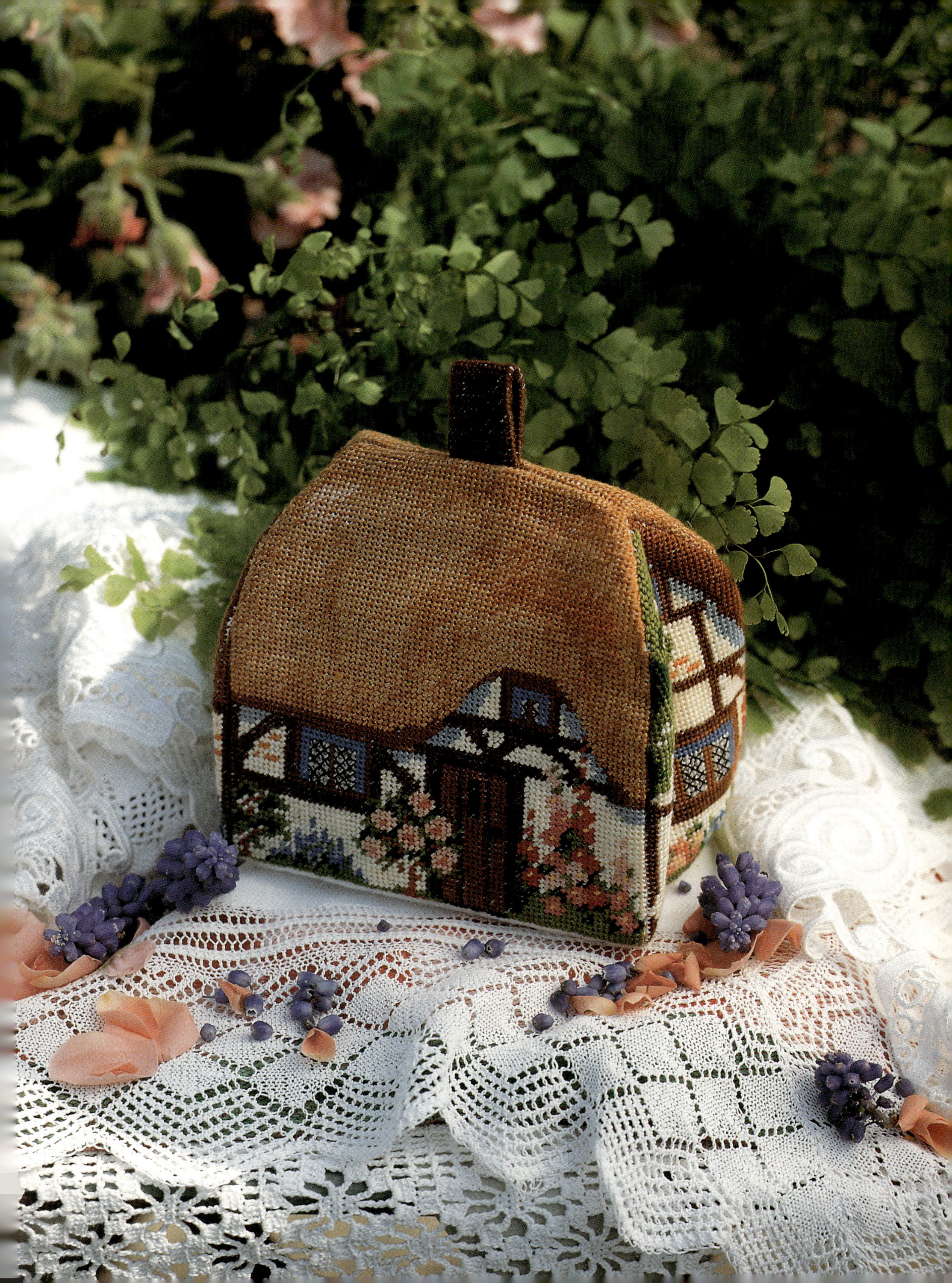

● 801	● 702	╱ 434	● 794	● 415	● 310	╱ 899	● 909	● 335	● 818	● 742
● 970	● 352	● 744	✕ 754	436x2 738x1	✕ 798	● 208	╱ 210	● 321	✕ 300	738x2 436x1
● 912	✕ 353	■ 351	□ 746							

Country Cottage Pot Pourri
(Above) back;
(Opposite) front

5 Trim the edges of the canvas to ¼in (5mm) from the stitching.
6 With right sides of the front and back of the cottage facing, sew the two rooftops together leaving a gap of ¾in (20mm) in the centre for the chimney (see diagram).
7 One by one, insert the cottage sides, pin them in place, and sew them up starting at the bottom and working up to the roof. Clip the curves carefully with a very sharp pair of scissors after stitching.
8 Turn the cottage right side out. Gently ease out the corners and fold the bottom edges under.
9 Make a small muslin pot pourri bag and place it inside the cottage. Plump the cottage out with wadding, but do not overfill.
10 Oversew around the edges of the piece of white felt to cover the bottom opening.

Country Cottage Pot Pourri
(Above) left side;
(Opposite) right side

11 For the chimney cut a piece of canvas 2½ x 1½in (63 x 38mm). Tent stitch using dark brown 801. Leave a border ¼in (5mm) all around.
12 Fold the chimney in half widthwise. Fold the canvas edges under and sew the sides together. Then fold in half lengthwise to make a loop.
13 Slot the chimney into the gap left in the roof and blindstitch in place.

DMC	COLOUR	ANCHOR
300	Rusty Brown	352
798	Blue	131
801	Dark Brown	359
794	Pale Blue	129
434	Brown	371
702	Bright Green	226
912	Mid Green	205
909	Dark Green	923
321	Burgundy	47
351	Dark Peach	10

DMC	COLOUR	ANCHOR	DMC	COLOUR	ANCHOR
352	Peach	9	310	Black	403
353	Pale Peach	8	738	Pale Ochre (2 skeins)	942
754	Very Pale Peach	6	436	Dark Ochre (2 skeins)	943
744	Yellow	295	415	Grey	398
208	Purple	111	742	Gold	303
210	Pale Purple	109	746	Cream background	386
899	Pink	52			
335	Dark Pink	41			
818	Pale Pink	48			
970	Orange	316			

CHAPTER 7

SPECIAL OCCASIONS AND MEMENTOES

It is always a pleasure to make or receive a hand-made memento of a special occasion. Birthdays or anniversaries, Mother's Day or family celebrations can be recorded for ever in a needlepoint design personalised with initials, mottos or particular motifs relating to the day. This idea goes back many centuries when young girls learning to stitch made samplers using different stitches and including verses, alphabets and small stylised motifs of figures, animals and foliage. These pieces are much sought after today and are a wonderful record of days gone by.

Our celebration wreath of flowers can be used for many different occasions. Wedding anniversaries can be distinguished by using threads of the appropriate colour: gold, silver, ruby and so on. For birthdays you could stitch the full name of the person and a birth date using one of the alphabets in the book, and in any colour of your choice.

Our Home Sweet Home would make a lovely 'welcome' gift for someone moving to a new house. Rather than a motto, the house name or address could be stitched beneath. The flowers on the border of this design would also work well in shades of yellow and give the picture a real feeling of springtime.

A wedding provides the ideal opportunity to stitch a design in needlepoint and a country scene conjures up the feeling of a traditional wedding day. Names and dates can be worked in the colour of your choice. You could also include the name of the church if you have enough space. We have charted other ideas for borders on page 126. Several of these would work well round this design.

Wedding Sampler

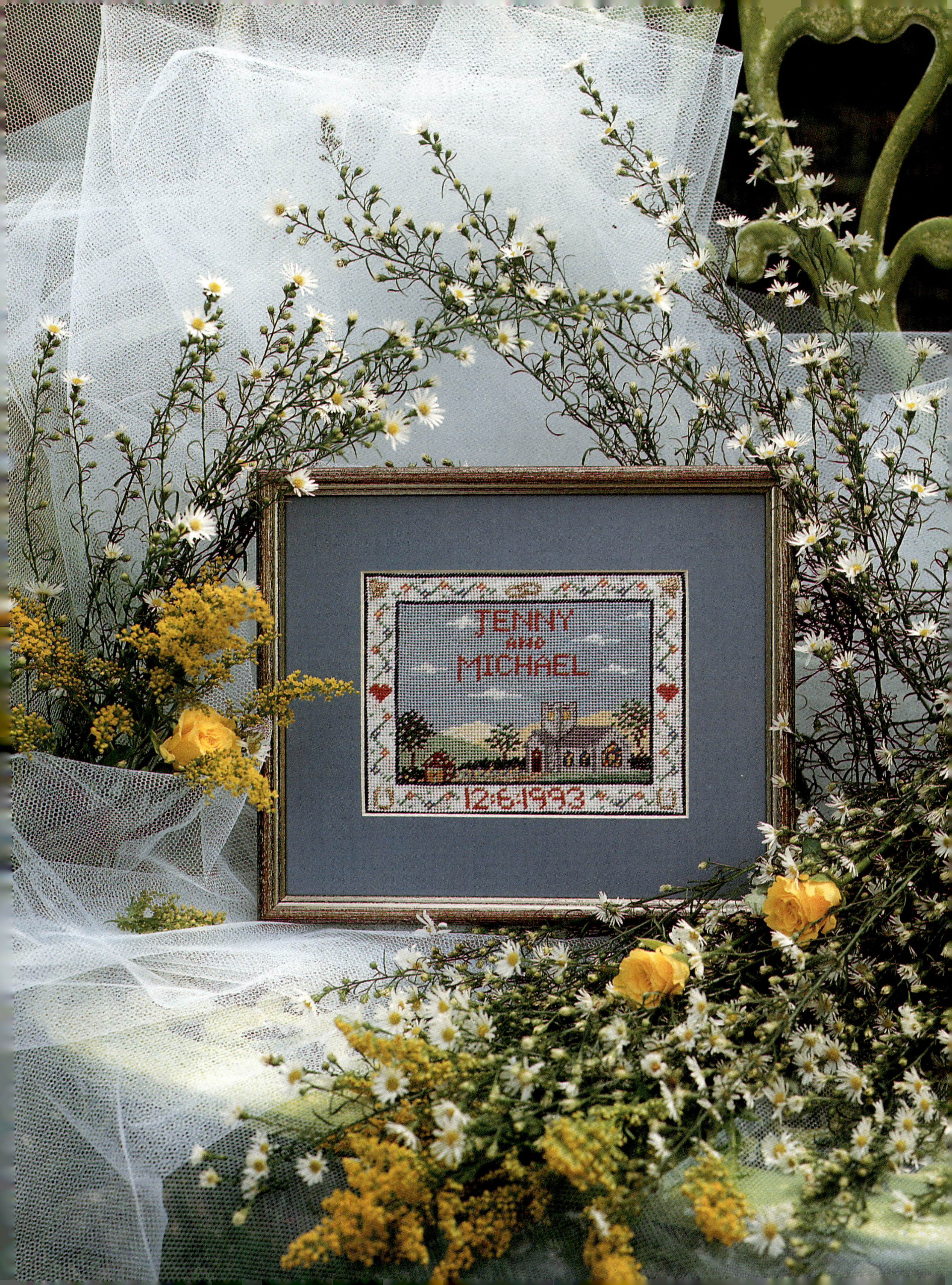

JENNY
and
MICHAEL
12·6·1993

WEDDING SAMPLER

This traditional wedding design shows a church set inside a delicate border of familiar marriage charms and tokens.

NEEDLE Size 22
CANVAS 18 holes to the inch (7 holes per cm)
SIZE OF CANVAS 7½ x 6¾in (190 x 170mm)
SIZE OF FINISHED DESIGN 5¾ x 4⅜in (145 x 110mm)

☐ Stranded cottons (floss) and metallic threads as listed on the chart key

Note This design is suitable for names up to 12 letters.

1 Find the centre point on the canvas and position the design as described in Basic Techniques.
2 Count the number of stitches to the inside border and work it first. Then work colour by colour from the centre point.
3 Use the alphabet on page 48 to make up the required names and date. Position the names and date as described in Basic Techniques and work them in the colour of your choice. To enlarge the first initial of each name, add 2 stitches to the letters on the chart.
4 To complete the design oversew the details of the church in backstitch using 1 strand of dark blue 336 for the windows; 1 strand of black 310 for the top of the church tower and the roof pitch; 1 strand of dark grey 414 for the tower windows and the corner of the tower.
5 To finish, work the outer border.
6 Mount and frame as preferred. Our sampler was mounted and framed professionally.

DMC	COLOUR	ANCHOR
319	Dark Green	212
800	Light Blue (2 skeins)	128
912	Mid Green	205
954	Light Green	203
700	Bright Green	228
3326	Pale Pink	25
335	Pink	41
309	Dark Pink	39
798	Mid Blue	131
743	Yellow	305
208	Purple	111
415	Light Grey	398
414	Dark Grey	400
336	Very Dark Blue	148
312	Dark Blue	147
300	Brown	352
676	Ochre	891
3032	Dark Beige	392
738	Light Beige	943
321	Burgundy	47
746	Light Cream	386
745	Dark Cream	300
310	Black	403
829	Dark Brown	906
Blanc	White (2 skeins)	01
MADEIRA	Metallic Gold	325

□	Blanc		
•	309	—	676
•	321	—	310
•	335	×	325 (Mad)
•	3326	•	800
•	743	•	312
•	954	•	208
•	912	×	798
•	700	/	738
×	414		
415x2 414x1			
•	415	•	746
•	300	•	319
•	336	—	829

103

HOME SWEET HOME

The photograph on page 89 shows a tiny cottage with roses clambering up whitewashed walls. On page 105 is a chart depicting a brick house with a flower garden and a white fence. Either design can be used inside the border of flowers on the chart on pages 106–107. Other mottoes are also charted or you can work your own using any of the alphabets in the book.

NEEDLE Size 22
CANVAS 18 holes to the inch (7 holes per cm)
SIZE OF CANVAS 9 x 9½in (230 x 240mm)
SIZE OF FINISHED DESIGN 5¾ x 6½in (145 x 165mm)
☐ Stranded cottons (floss) as listed on the chart key

1 Find the centre point on the canvas and position the design as described in Basic Techniques.
2 Count the number of stitches from the centre point to the inside border around the cottage. Work it first, then work colour by colour from the centre point.
3 Work the house and porch roofs, window and door frames, and the chimney in brick stitch. Outline the flower petals using backstitch in 1 strand of burgundy 321.
4 Using 1 strand of black 310 for the porch and 1 strand of grey 415 for the door panels, outline in backstitch as shown. Oversew lattice on the windows on the front door with 1 strand of white.
5 If you decide to insert the brick house, complete the design and outline the fence using 1 strand of dark grey 415. Outline the door and fascia boards using 1 strand of black 310. Outline pink flowers using 1 strand of burgundy 321.

DMC	COLOUR	ANCHOR
Home Sweet Home		
433	Brown	371
436	Ochre	943
699	Dark Green	923
702	Green	226
772	Pale Green	253
794	Pale Blue	129
798	Blue	131
208	Purple	110
210	Pale Purple	109
321	Burgundy	47
801	Dark Brown	359
310	Black	403
415	Dark Grey	398
742	Gold	303
3326	Pale Pink	25
899	Pink	52
335	Dark Pink	41
317	Light Grey	400
Blanc	White	01
746	Cream background (3 skeins)	386
Red Brick House		
920	Brick Red	340
922	Pale Brick Red	338
321	Burgundy	47
772	Pale Green	253
702	Green	226
798	Blue	131
800	Pale Blue	128
209	Purple	110
436	Ochre	943
300	Brown	352
317	Grey	400
415	Dark Grey	398
310	Black	403
742	Gold	303
743	Yellow	305
899	Pink	52
Blanc	White	01

• 922	• 300	• 321	• 743	• 310	• 317	∕ 436
• 899	• 800	• 798	• 702	• 742	• 772	× 209
• 920	— 415	— 920	☐ Blanc			

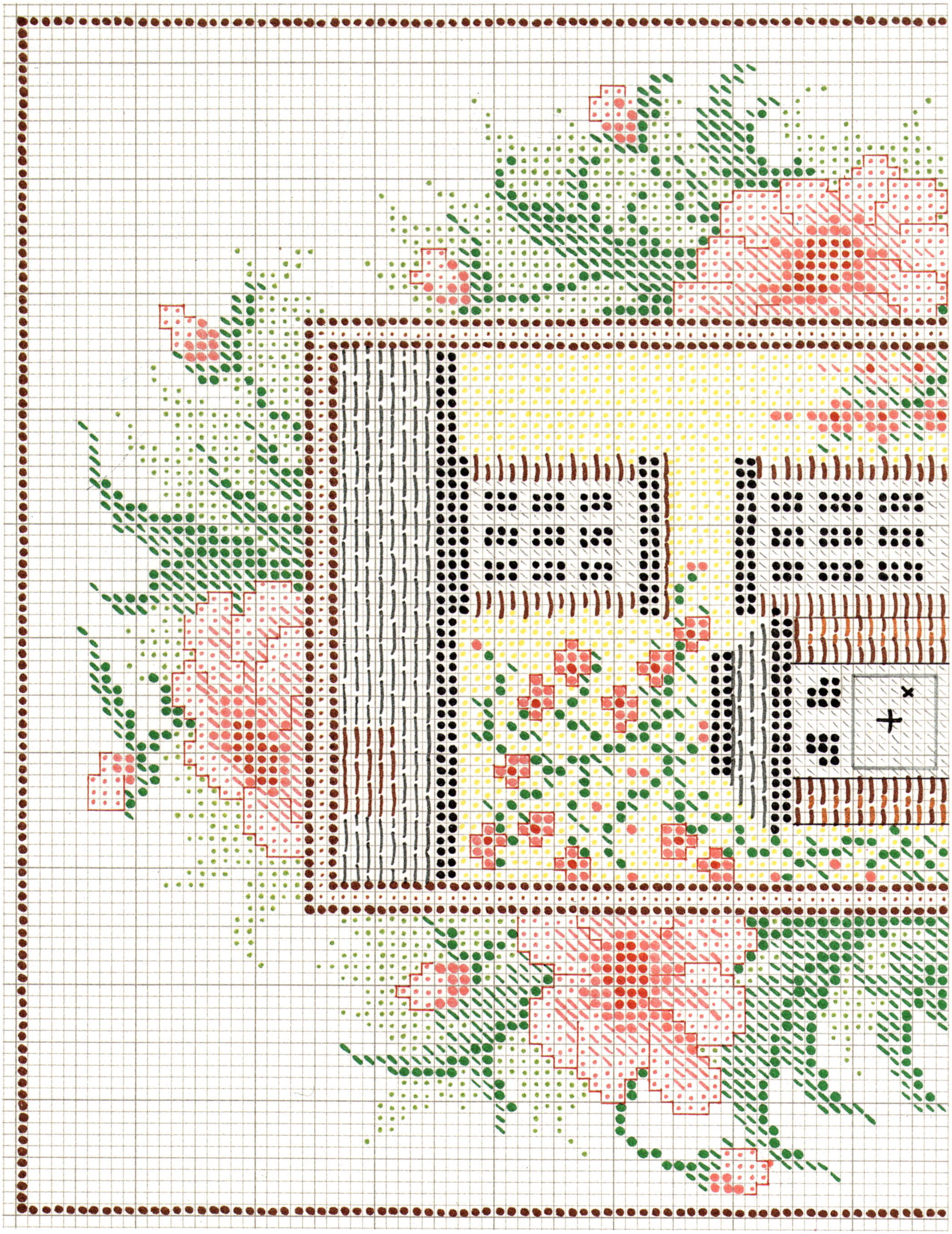

Home Sweet Home
Alternative Mottoes

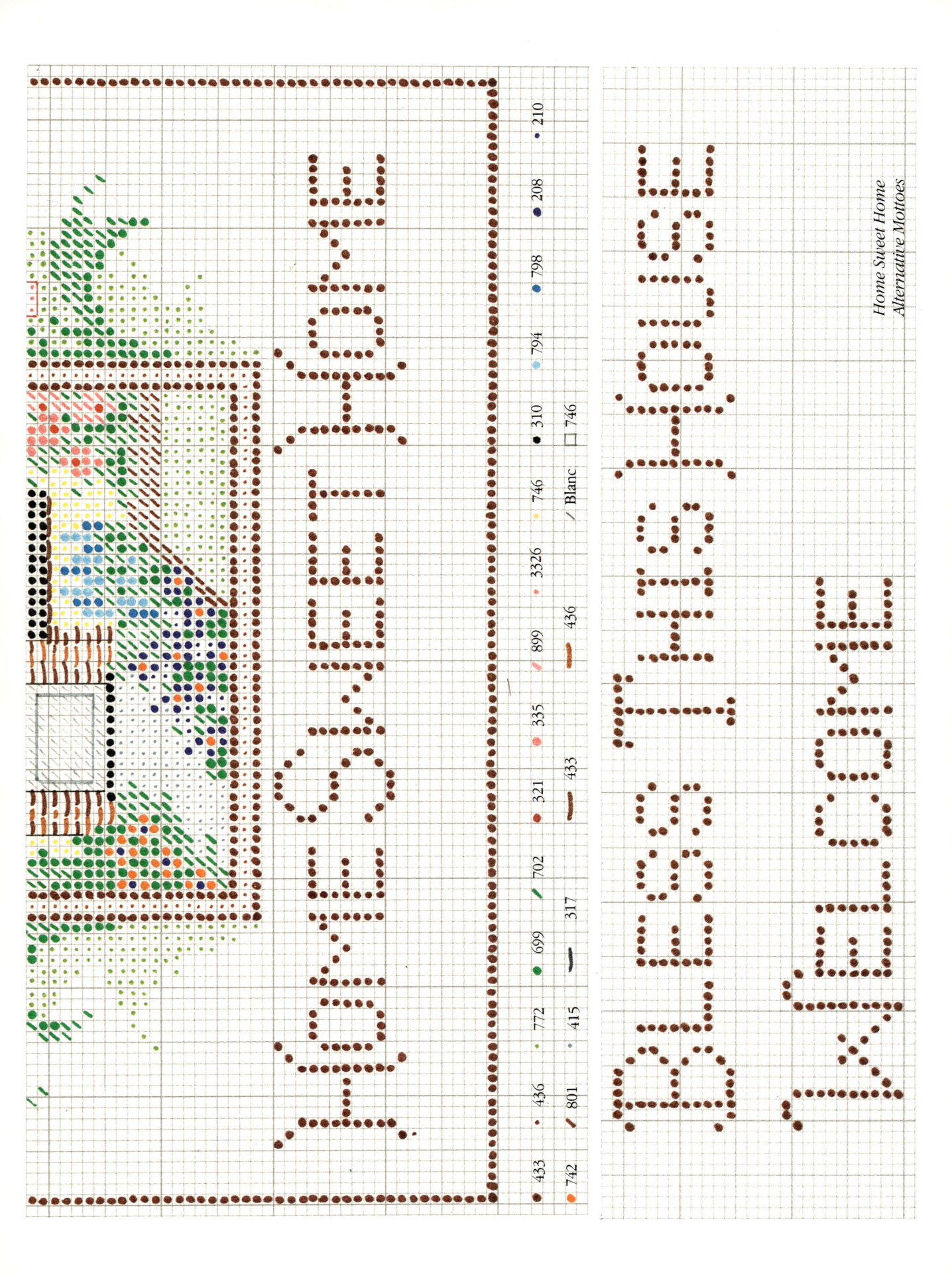

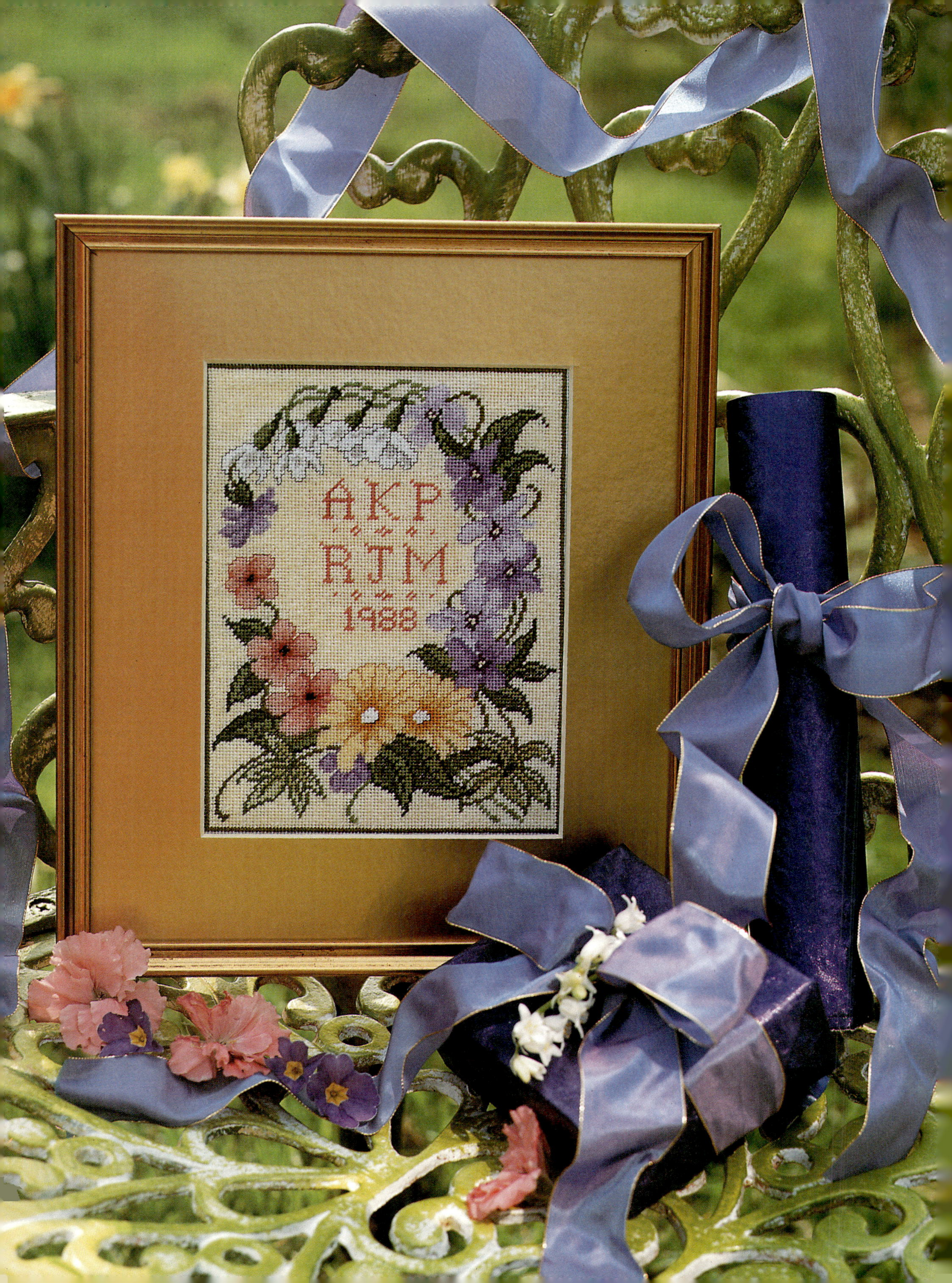
AKP
RJM
1988

CELEBRATION FLORAL WREATH

In this pretty design, suitable for any special occasion, violets, daisies, snowdrops and campions in an oval garland encircle the decorative initials.

NEEDLE Size 22
CANVAS 18 holes to the inch (7 holes per cm)
SIZE OF CANVAS 9 x 11in (230 x 280mm)
SIZE OF FINISHED DESIGN 5¾ x 8in (145 x 203mm)
□ Stranded cottons (floss) and cotton perlé (pearl cottons) as listed on chart key

1 Find the centre point on the canvas and position the design as described in Basic Techniques.
2 As the centre of this design comes in an area of background colour, choose a flower to start with and count the number of stitches from the centre point to the flower.
3 Work the flowers and leaves first colour by colour. Use 1 strand of burgundy 321 and backstitch to outline the pink flowers. Use 1 strand of dark grey 317 to outline the snowdrops and 1 strand of gold 782 to outline the daisies. Use 1 strand of dark purple 208 to outline the violets ONLY where shown on the chart.
4 For the initials, choose one of the alphabets in the book. The date can be included using the number chart on page 48.
5 Our project was professionally mounted in an old gold frame with a striking gold mount.
NB Perlé thread 3347 is marked (P) on chart to differentiate it from stranded cotton 3347.

DMC	COLOUR	ANCHOR
550	Very Dark Purple	102
936	Dark Green	846
745	Cream	300
3346	Mid Green	267
783	Light Gold	306
471	Light Green	255
209	Purple	110
211	Pale Purple	108
3347	Green	266
782	Gold	307
772	Pale Green	253
208	Dark Purple	111
210	Light Purple	109
310	Black	403
415	Light Grey	398
317	Dark Grey	400
321	Burgundy	47
335	Dark Pink	41
899	Pink	52
3326	Light Pink	25
676	Pale Gold	891
Blanc	White	01
746	Cream background (3 skeins)	386
3347	Green Perlé No. 5	266
937	Mid Green Perlé No. 5	269

Floral Wreath

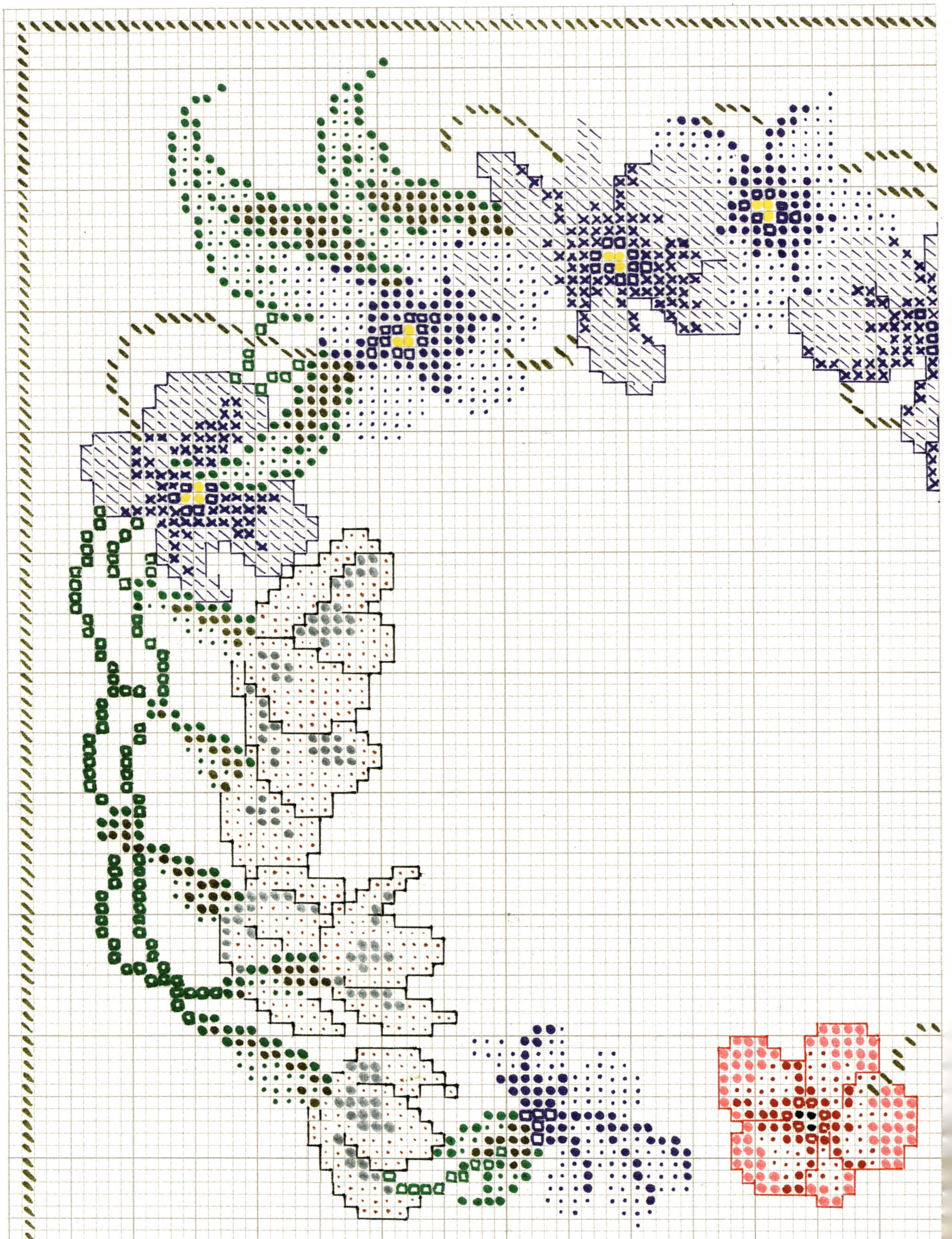

● 936	● 3347	● 937	● 471	● 3347(P)	● 208	× 210	/ 211	— 317
● 3326	● 3346	● 321	● 745	● 209	● 676	● 310	□ 746
	● 899	● 335	● 782	● Blanc	● 783	● 415	□ 550
						772

Celebration Floral Wreath

CHAPTER 8

EXOTICA

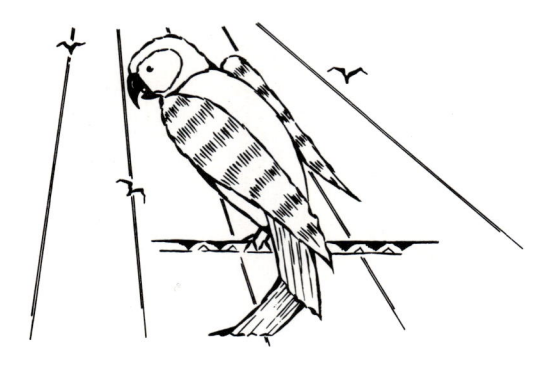

DISTANT places have provided the theme for the pieces in this chapter. Travelling is a wonderful stimulus, particularly to the keen eye of the would-be designer. When we visit different cultures we become aware of different, perhaps more vibrant, use of colour and this may make us more adventurous with our own choices.

The Blue Macaw on his perch is bathing in rays of sunshine. The stained glass panels of the Art Deco period, which can still be seen in doorways and porches in many places, have provided the influence.

The colours have been allowed to run riot in the rich Tropical Cushion with its palm trees and sailing boats. Different stitches create depth and movement in the trees and on the water. The oranges and golds are warm colours, reminiscent of sunny days.

Tropical Fish is a very delicate and rather special piece. This is a 'copy' – with a few minor adjustments. The original design is from a pair of 19th-century Chinese sleevebands. Worked on very fine silk gauze using silk threads, they were part of a lady's summer robe. The workmanship is exquisite, and we have attempted to capture some of the original beauty.

To cooler climates for the little Penguin Picture. Sitting on the ice floe, these are just for fun. Animals generally are not easy to work realistically in fine needlepoint. It is better to choose an animal that can be stylised or look humorous. We have attempted dogs and horses which have turned out looking like space invaders!

Blue Macaw

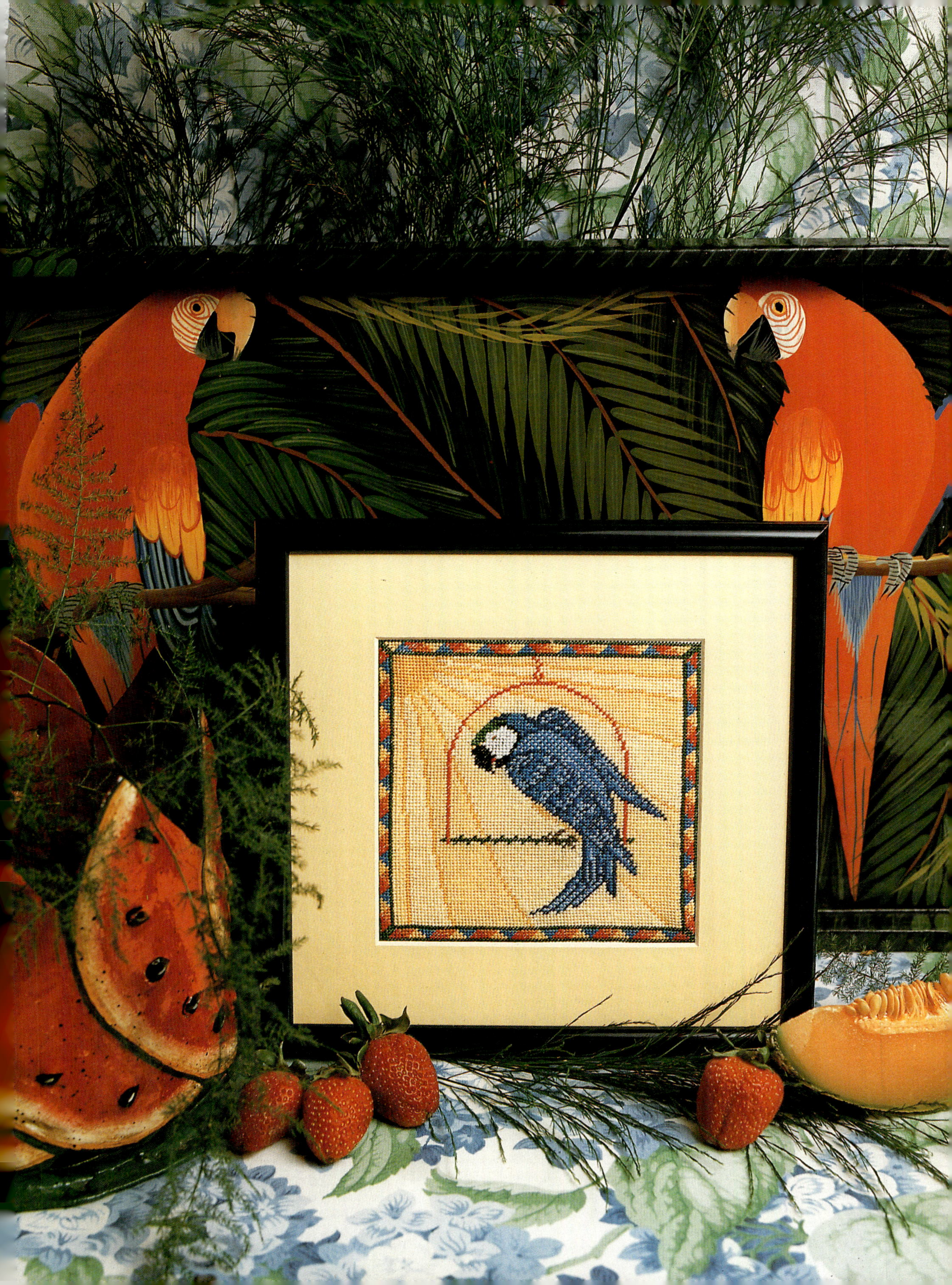

BLUE MACAW

The vibrant colours of the tropics and the simple style of the Art Deco period are both captured in this piece.

NEEDLE Size 22
CANVAS 18 holes per inch (7 holes per cm)
SIZE OF CANVAS 9 x 9in (230 x 230mm)
SIZE OF FINISHED DESIGN 5¼ x 5¼in (134 x 134mm)
☐ Stranded cottons (floss) as listed on the chart key

1 Find the centre point on the canvas and position the design as described in Basic Techniques.
2 Count from the centre point to the bird's black beak and start stitching here. Stitch the rest of the bird and the perch, working colour by colour.
3 Stitch the patterned border.
4 Stitch the background sunrays, segment by segment.
5 This picture was professionally mounted and framed in dark blue lacquered wood that brings out the dark blue in the macaw's feathers.

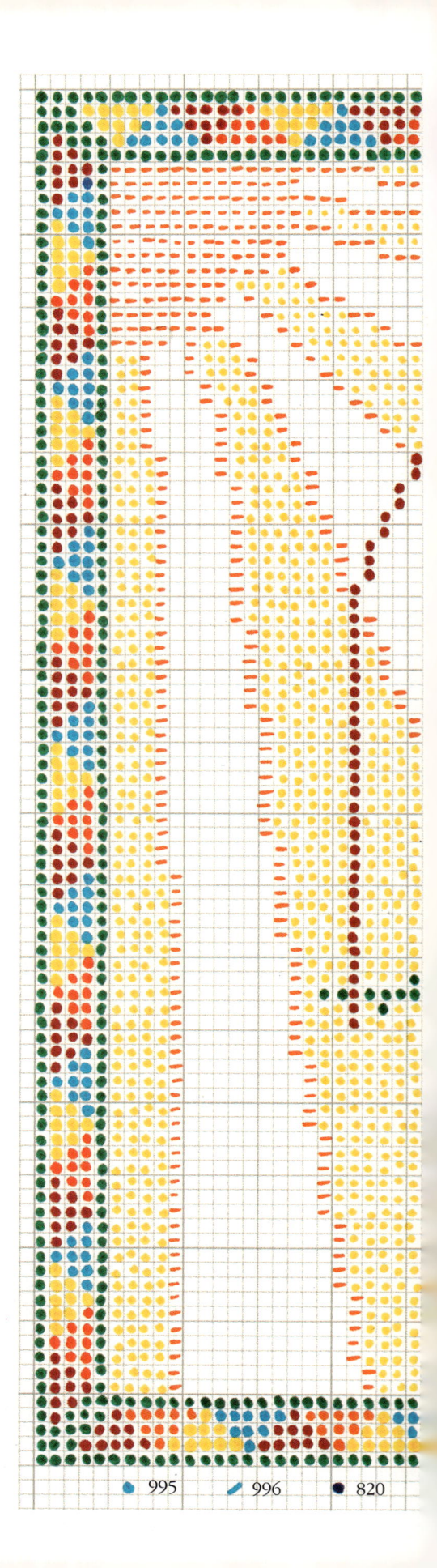

DMC	COLOUR	ANCHOR
995	Turquoise	410
996	Light Turquoise	433
820	Navy Blue	134
699	Green	923
666	Red	46
720	Orange	326
310	Black	403
610	Brown	889
742	Dark Yellow	303
743	Yellow	305
744	Pale Yellow (2 skeins)	295
745	Dark Cream (2 skeins)	300
Blanc	White	01

| 743 | 744 | 720 | — 742 | 666 | 699 | 310 | 610 | Blanc | □ 745 |

TROPICAL CUSHION

This exotic cushion, particularly suited to a sunny conservatory, will brighten up any room.

NEEDLE Size 20
CANVAS 14 holes to the inch (5½ holes per cm)
SIZE OF CANVAS 18 x 14in (460 x 360mm)
SIZE OF FINISHED DESIGN 12½ x 9¾in (315 x 247mm)
☐ Stranded cottons (floss) as listed in the chart key
☐ Backing fabric 18 x 14in (460 x 360mm)
☐ Cushion pad 12 x 9½in (300 x 240mm)

1   Find the centre point on the canvas and position the design as described in Basic Techniques.
2   Count the number of stitches from the centre point to the purple door of the orange house and start stitching here, then work colour by colour.
3   For the palm trees stitch the tent stitch outlines first and then fill in with vertical brick stitch.
4   Stitch the sailboats before filling in the blue sea background in horizontal brick stitch.
5   Stitch the outside border in sloping Gobelin stitch.
6   Block the needlepoint and make up the cushion as described on page 57.

DMC	COLOUR	ANCHOR
602	Pink (3 skeins)	77
600	Dark Pink	65
823	Navy (3 skeins)	150
909	Dark Green (3 skeins)	923
912	Mid Green	205
907	Lime Green (3 skeins)	255
906	Dark Lime Green (2 skeins)	256
970	Orange (3 skeins)	316
742	Gold (4 skeins)	303
996	Blue (8 skeins)	433
680	Dark Ochre	901
208	Purple	110
Blanc	White (3 skeins)	01

Tropical Cushion

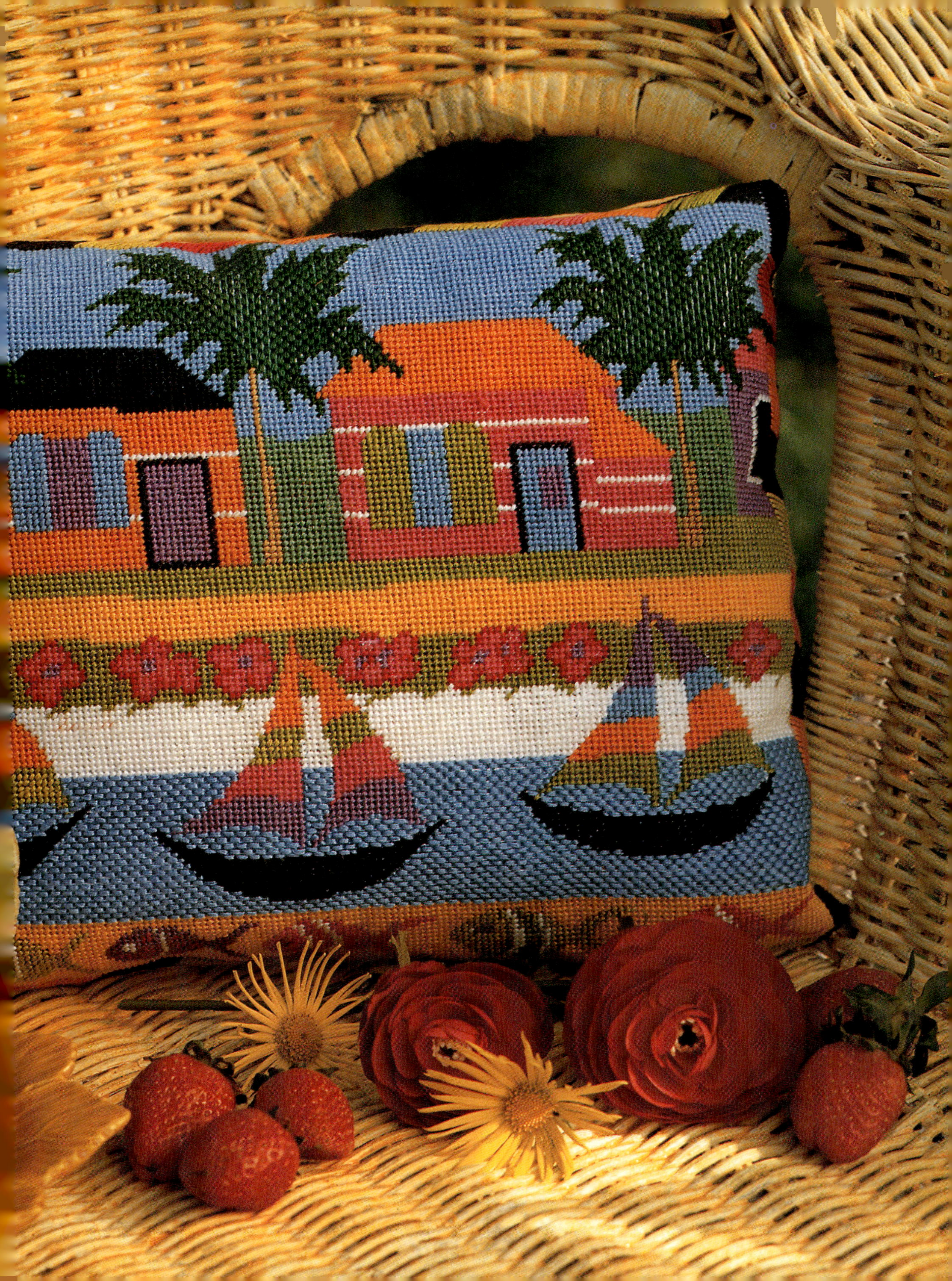

118

| Blanc
| 208
| 996
| 909
| 912
| 602
| 600
| 907
| 906
| 680
| 970
| 742
| 823

Tropical cushion left side

120

□	Blanc
•	208
—	996
—	909
/	912
•	602
•	600
•	907
•	906
•	680
•	970
•	742
•	823

Tropical cushion right side

ORIENTAL FISH

Exquisitely embroidered sleevebands from an antique Chinese robe were the inspiration for this underwater scene (see photograph on page 7).

NEEDLE Size 22
CANVAS 18 holes per inch (7 holes per cm)
SIZE OF CANVAS 8 x 12in (200 x 305mm)
SIZE OF FINISHED DESIGN 3⅞ x 8⅛in (98 x 206mm)
☐ Stranded cottons (floss) as listed on the chart key

1 Find the centre point on the canvas and position the design as described in Basic Techniques.
2 Count from the centre point to the head of the peach fish. Start stitching the border of the fish and then fill in the shading. Stitch the blue fish.
3 Stitch the flowers and water lines, then fill in the cream background.
4 Work French knots where indicated by a circle on the chart, using three strands of peach 352.

5 This project was professionally mounted in soft blue and framed in an old gold frame with a border line of the same blue.

DMC	COLOUR	ANCHOR
336	Dark Blue	148
798	Mid Blue	131
794	Blue	129
800	Pale Blue	128
775	Very Pale Blue	158
772	Pale Green	253

DMC	COLOUR	ANCHOR
3348	Green	265
3347	Dark Green	266
310	Black	403
349	Dark Peach	13
351	Mid Peach	11
352	Peach	9
353	Pale Peach	8
746	Cream background (3 skeins)	386

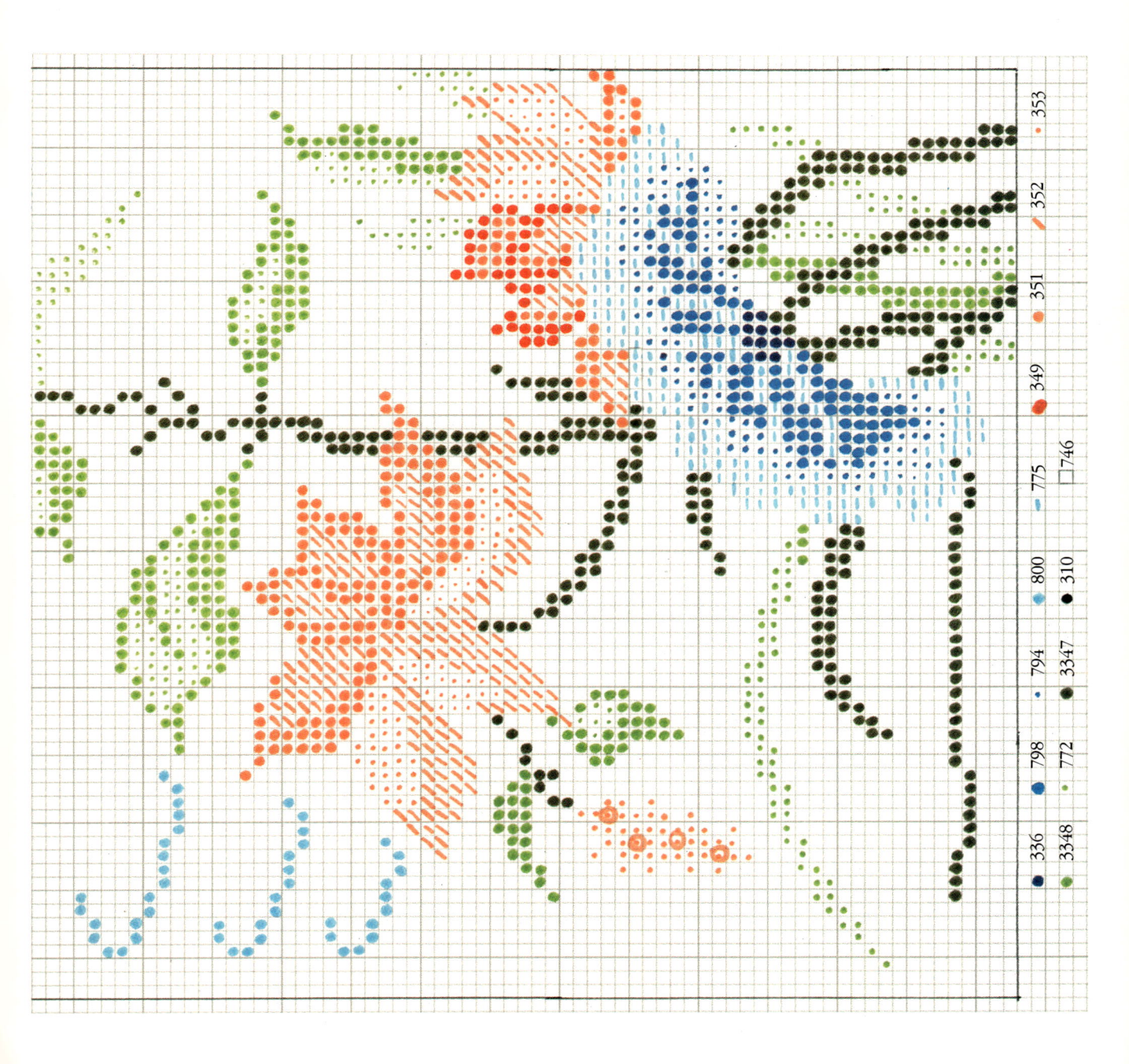

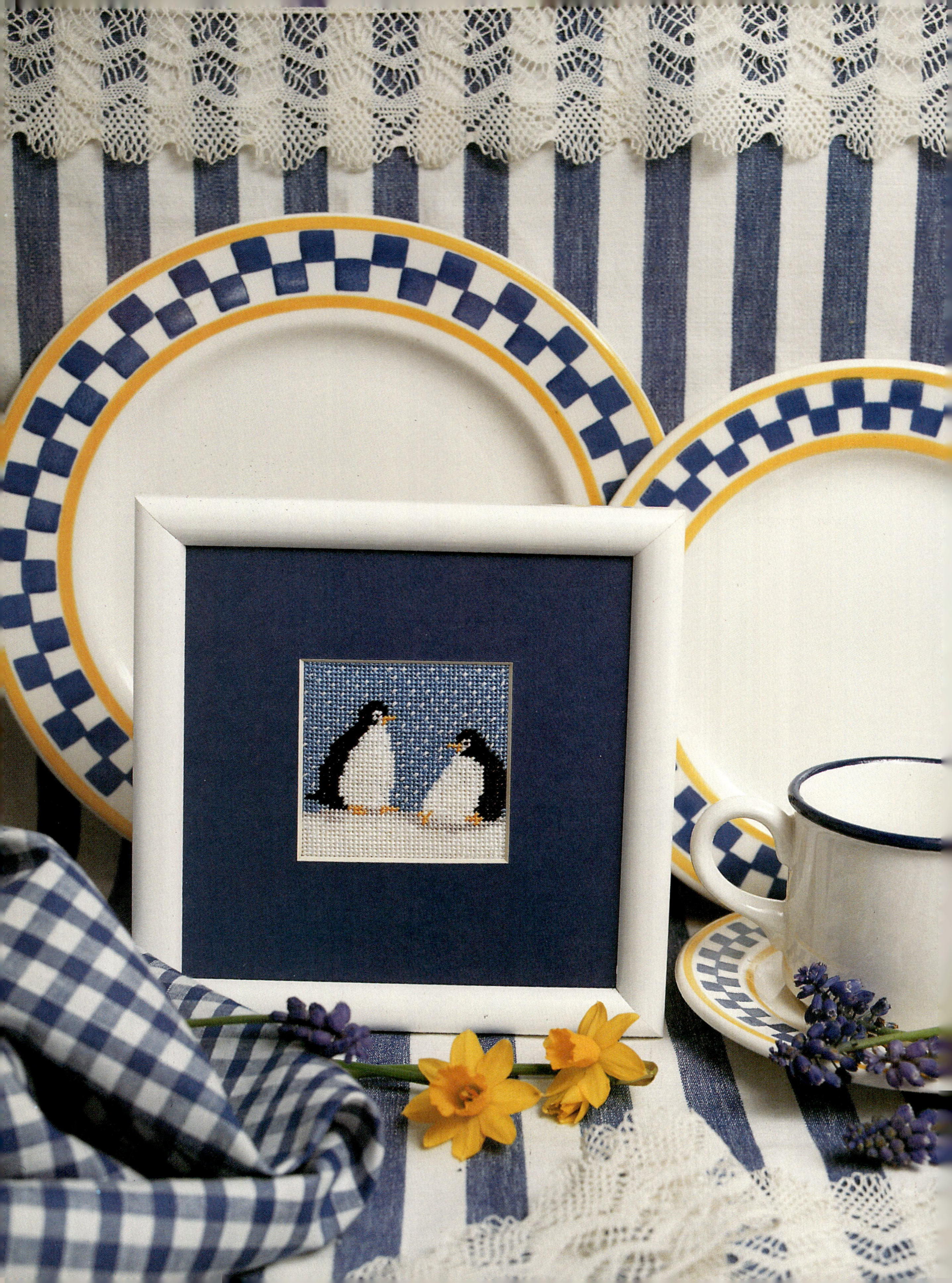

Two Plump Penguins

These friendly penguins look cool in any room.

NEEDLE Size 22
CANVAS 18 holes to the inch (7 holes per cm)
SIZE OF CANVAS 5 x 5in (125 x 125mm)
SIZE OF FINISHED DESIGN 2½ x 2½in (64 x 64mm)
☐ Stranded cottons (floss) as listed on chart key

1 Find the centre point on the canvas and position the design as described in Basic Techniques.
2 Count the number of stitches from the centre point to one of the penguins heads and start stitching here. Work colour by colour, leaving the white areas until last.
3 Using 1 strand of black 310 work a French knot to make each penguin's eye.
4 Our penguins have been professionally mounted and framed in blue and white, but would fit nicely into a 3-fold card with a 2½in (64mm) square window, following the instructions for mounting cards in Basic Techniques.

DMC	COLOUR	ANCHOR
Blanc	White	01
310	Black	403
798	Blue	131
742	Gold	303
415	Grey	398

Plump Penguins

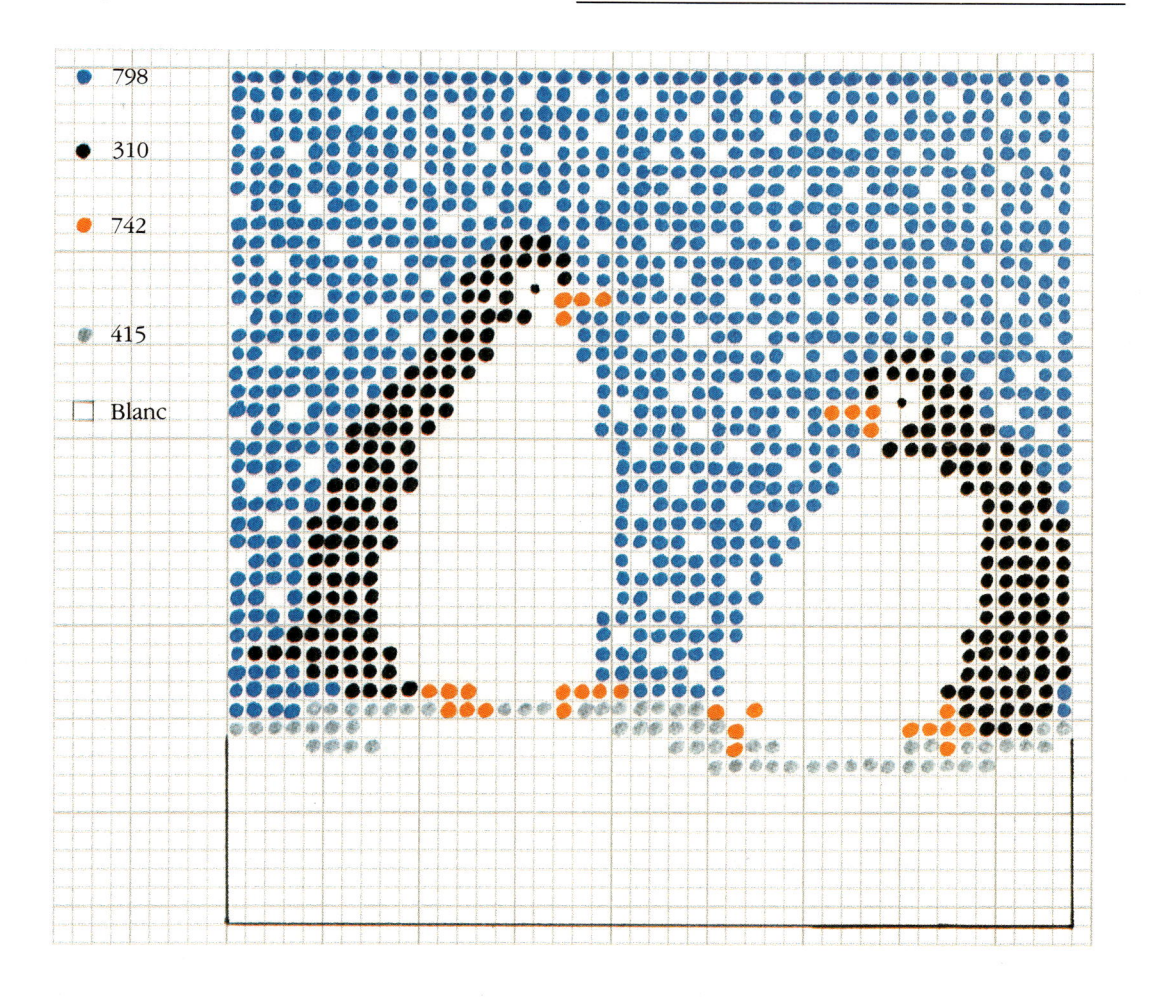

Borders and Alphabets

ABCDEFG
HIJKLMN
OPQRSTU
VWXYZ

ABCDEFGHIJ
KLMNOPQRS
TUVWXYZ
1234567890

INDEX

Figures in *italic* refer to illustrations

alphabets, 14, 126–7; Alphabet Cushion, 46, 57–61, *60*
animal designs, 112

backstitch, 13, 14
Benjamin's Sampler, *2, 47,* 54–5
birthday greeting cards, 20–5
Black Cat on Windowledge, *17,* 18
blocking, 14–15
Blue Macaw, *113,* 114–15
borders, 126; Floral Frame, 86–7, *85*
bows; Christmas Bow, 32–5, *31*; Hair Bow, 92–3, *92*; Picture Bow, 88–91, *89*
brick stitch, 12–13, 14
Butterfly Needlecase/Pincushion, 78–9, 80–3

Canterbury Bells, *67,* 68–9
canvas, 9
Cat on a Windowledge, *17,* 18
Celebration Floral Wreath, *108,* 109–11
Christmas themes, 30–45
cotton perlé, 10, 66
Country Cottage Pot Pourri, 94–9, *95*
Country Scene, 19, *21*
cushions; Alphabet Cushion, 46, 57–61, *60*; Tropical Cushion, 116–19, *116–17*

decorative ideas, 84–99
Door Plaque, 52–3, *56*

Emma's Swans and Rabbits, 50–1
equipment, 9–10
exotica, 112–25

Father Christmas card, 44, *42–3*
floss, 10
flower designs; Canterbury Bells, *67,* 68–9; Celebration Floral Wreath, *108,* 109–11; Floral Frame, *85,* 86–7; floral motifs, 84; Pansy, 70, *72–3*; Pink Poppy Tile, *72–3,* 74–6; Red Campion, 71, *72–3*; Victorian Posy Box, 78–9, *78*
frames; framing and mounting, 14–15; picture frames, 84–7; tapestry frames, 10
French knots, 13, 14

Georgian Country House, 20–1, *21*
Gobelin stitch, 13
Good Luck card, 18
graph paper, 10; graphing letters and numbers, 14
greetings cards, 16–29; Christmas themes, 39–44

Hair Bow, 92–3, *92*
Happy Birthday card, *24,* 25
Heartfelt Greetings, 23, *24*
Ho! Ho! Ho!, *42–3,* 44
Hollyhocks, *21,* 22
Home Sweet Home, *89,* 100, 104–7

Jennifer's Fairy, *47,* 48–9

letters of alphabet, 14, 127

materials, 9–10
mementoes, 100–11
metallic threads, 10
mirror mount, 84, 86
Mother's Day card, 22
mounting and framing, 14–15

needlecase, 78–9, 80–2
needles, 9
new baby; New Arrival card, 26–7, *27*; nursery pictures, 46–51
numbers, 14, 48
nursery themes, 46–65

Oriental Fish, 7, 122–3
oversewing, 13

Pansy, 70, *72–3*
pearl cotton, 10, 66
Penelope (canvas), 9
Penguin Picture, 112, 124–5, *124*
photograph frame, 84–7
Picture Bow, 88–91, *89*
picture frames, 84–7
pincushion, 78–9, 81, 83
Pink Poppy Tile, *72–3,* 74–6
pot pourri, 84, 94–9

Red Campion, 71, *72–3*
ribbons, 16, 88
Robin on a Snowy Bough, *31,* 32–3

samplers, 46, 50–1, 100; Benjamin's Sampler, *2, 47,* 54–5; Emma's Swans and Rabbits, 50–1; Teddy Bear's Picnic, 62–5, *65*; Wedding Sampler, *101,* 102–3
scissors, 10
special occasions, 100–11
stitches, 11–13, 14

Teddy and Balloons, 28–9
Teddy Bear's Picnic, 62–5, *65*
tent stitch, 12, 14
Thatched Cottage, *67,* 76–7
threads, 10, 11; colour coding, 14; cotton perlé, 10, 66
Thumbelina Designs, 8, 46
Tropical Cushion, *116–17,* 116–19
Twinkling Star, 36–7, *38*

Victorian treasures, 66–83

Wedding Sampler, *101,* 102–3